Reflections of Trethurgy

In

Words and Pictures

*Maggie Roberts, Mabel Seward
& Barrie Shipley*

First Edition and Published in 2014

Tamerisk Publications
Trethurgy
St Austell
Cornwall
PL26 8YD

Cover Design and Typesetting by Malcolm Roberts

Printed by Nationwide Print
Holmbush, St Austell, Cornwall PL25 3JL
01726 72548

ISBN 978 0 9929463 0 2

<u>Dedication</u>

In this, the centenary anniversary of the outbreak of the First World War (1914 - 1918), this book is dedicated to Private Edwin James Burt, who was killed in action in the fields of Flanders on the 11th April 1916; and to the many other brave men who responded to the call of duty and nobly sacrificed their lives.

Private Burt, of 7th Battalion of the Duke of Cornwall Light Infantry, was the first man from Trethurgy to lay down his life for King and Country.

Acknowledgements

In writing this book, we wish to extend our grateful appreciation to a number of people for their support and valued contributions; be it in lending us photographs or, in their written recordings of life in Trethurgy. Whilst some of the contributors still live locally; others, have moved away, but continue to hold a special place in their hearts for this small hamlet and community.

Louella Hanbury-Tennison
Alec Hambly
Marjorie Hambly
Valerie Hicks
Margaret Hocking
Valerie & Brian Jacob
Marian & Mick Johnson
Sarah Mears & Mark Truscott
Jean Niles

Dennis Ronaldson
RNAS Culdrose
Mabel & Tom Seward
Barrie Shipley
Sheila Thorn
John Tonkin
Jackie Trudgeon
Kathryn Wells
Shirley Wooders

We are especially indebted to Tom Seward; for without his numerous old newspaper cuttings, photographs and many anecdotal memories of his life over the past fifty or so years, this book would not have been possible.

We further convey our thanks to the staff of the Cornwall Record Office in Truro and the Courtney Library at Truro Museum, for their help and support.

The Sir Arthur Quiller
Couch Memorial Fund

Contents

Introduction

Tom and I arrived in Trethurgy in 1959. It was a rather bleak and sparse village, but the welcome we received from the folk living here at the time was inviting and genuine. We have seen the village life change and have many memories of a bygone age.

The changes started when the Treverbyn estate sold off the leases to properties and various parcels of land back in the 1960s. The inhabitants, now being freeholders, had an incentive to update their properties and this was the beginning of the new development.

The village had its own shop and post office which was a little granite building at the back of Rockhurst. Kath Davidson was both the shopkeeper and postmistress. She was a warm hearted lady and her shop was the centre of the community. Later, this building was demolished and a new one built which was attached to their house. When the Davidsons retired to a bungalow built in their garden, the Mugford family moved into Rockhurst, with Mrs Mugford running the shop and post office business until it closed in August 1987.

At the time of our moving into the village, there were nine working farms or smallholdings, namely: Trethurgy Farm (occupied by the Kingdon family); Knightor Farm (Luke); Alseveor Farm (Cook); Penhedra (Nancarrow); Carn Grey (Croucher); Chytan (Martin); Hills (Hambly); Grey (Croucher) and Little Grey (Minear). These smallholdings were usually run alongside another job; often, that of shift work in the clay industry.

The clay industry was mainly responsible for changing the way of life and local landscape when it started excavating within the area. Knightor, Penhedra, Alseveor and part of Trethurgy Farm were all victims of the developing industry. Fortunately, in the 1970s, the clay company allowed an archaeological dig to take place on land off Butts Lane. This dig was to avail some very early history dating back to 400 AD. Later, the area was to be covered with sand waste.

Harold Hambly from Hills Farm delivered our milk. His tractor could be heard 'ticking over' all around the village for most of the morning as he did his round and had a neighbourly chat. Later, Diana Martin from Chytan delivered our milk in a little trolley which she pushed around.

The bread was delivered three times a week from Eustace Bakery in St Austell; whilst our butcher, Joe Kittow from St Blazey, would call on Mondays and Fridays. Mr Golly from Tregrehan Post Office and stores also made deliveries; as did Mr Rowett, who kept a grocery shop in Tregrehan. The Royal Mail postal deliveries would take place both in the mornings and afternoons.

There were only a few cars in the village at that time, but this didn't seem to matter. The community was very close and united if anyone ever needed help or an emergency situation arose. There was also a bus service which ran through the village from St Austell to Luxulyan three times a day. On Saturdays, there was also a late bus so that people could go to the cinema in the town.

The chapel was both the spiritual and social centre of our local community. The village children went to the Sunday School and the celebrations for feast days, harvest and Christmas were always popular and well attended. Sadly, as the chapel congregations dwindled and the overhead running costs increased, it was forced to close in 1985.

Following this, the village activites centred more around the village hall, with our grateful thanks and appreciation going to the long standing committee who have given many years of service to improving and keeping the only remaining community interest going. It has seen various events taking place there, including the Flower Show which was previously held in the Sunday school room. Local fetes and fun sports were also very popular on the playing field, with the entertainment being provided by what was affectionately called the 'Trethurgy All Star Band'. The enthusiasm for this band centred around Peter Minear. He was a talented player and could always rally a few players to make a good sound. Sadly, Peter lost his battle with cancer in 2008. Following in his tradition, we are most grateful to his daughter, Anna, and son, Ben, for keeping this musical custom going. My Tom and his euphonium always enjoyed being part of these events.

During recent times, Katherine Wright and Avril Moyle, together with some of their friends, have organised the 'Parties in the Park.' These successful events have helped to raise funds to support the village hall, the playing field and other charities.

It has been difficult to find much recorded history about Trethurgy, but interest grew following a conversation we had with Margaret and Malcolm Roberts. They had moved into the village in 1997 and were interested to learn more about their new surroundings. Tom agreed for them to look through his memorabilia which he has collected for more than half a century. These include postcards and photos of many social and religious occasions; past employment in the area; the neighbourhood landscape and of the many local characters. He has a good memory and recalls lots of stories which the village folk would tell.

I should like to pay retrospective thanks to my late mother, Kathleen Hawke, who liked to be around and about with her camera taking photographs. Also, for her collection of written accounts which have helped to make us more aware of the changing times.

When Margaret retired from teaching at Tywardreath School, her interest grew to place Tom's historic memorabilia in some form of chronological order. Enlisting the help and enthusiasm of Barrie Shipley, who grew up in the village, further helped to spur us on. He was able to draw in more people who lived here during the 1940-50s to recall their memories.

Many hours of chatting and numerous cups of tea were to follow as their reminiscenses unfolded. Independently, Margaret and Barrie did further research at the County Museum and Cornwall Record Office at Truro, with this being a somewhat difficult task since recorded mentions of Trethurgy are quite sparse. However, their findings have added further interest to this book.

Despite everyone's best effort, people's recollections are not always accurate. There may be differing thoughts and recollections but, to the best of our awareness, the presented pictures, referrals and memories recalling such times, are considered to be a true record and worthy of retention for posterity.

Mabel Seward

Early History

Trethurgy as a community was first recorded in AD1200 as *Tredeurgy* and formed part of the Treverbyn estate. Later, the spelling changed to *Tredoferi* with the name being derived from *'tre'* meaning 'farmstead or estate' and *'doferhi'*, meaning 'otter'. In the eighteenth century, it is noted from various documentations that the spelling had changed to *Trethurgey*.

Trethurgy in the early 1900s. This photo was taken looking towards the Kingdon's family farm. Below, is the same location in 2009.

High above the village is *Carn Grey* which is believed to have been occupied in Bronze Age times with legends of pagan rites having taken place there.

It is thought that those early people used the flat rock on top of the rocky outcrop for sun worshipping, and sculpted the stones below to make an anti-clockwise stairway to it.

The magical 'Carn Grey' as it looks in the 21st century.

It was also believed that between 700 and 200 BC, Phoenician traders conducted Baal worship there. Baal was the 'God of Weather and Storms' and also, associated with fertility. It was highly likely that the Phoenicians took advantage of the tidal outlet which came within three miles of modern Trethurgy. The Phoenicians were drawn to the Cornish coast for tin. It was usual for the merchants to trade skins and hides in return. They also traded pottery, salt and articles of bronze, such as weapons, tools and utensils for cooking and eating with.

A drawing of a typical Phoenician ship that would have regularly visited St Austell Bay on trading missions.

The Chapel

Trethurgy has had a place of worship since 1817, according to the deeds, which date back to 22nd August of that year. The original wood building was situated in *Knightor Lane*. Very little is known about the old chapel, apart from the fact that the roof was repaired in 1865, at a cost of £3/4/0d. We further know, from the old chapel records, that a meeting was held in June of that same year and attended by the Rev. Hardy, James Stephens, John Geach, Thomas Floyd, Joseph Hore, William Nicholls and B.D Julyan, to decide the fate of the old chapel. The outcome was to use the building as a school-room and this proposal was sent to the trustees of the chapel, along with the costs of the conversion which was £42. Much later on, in 1902, a letter was received from the Central Buildings for Wesleyan Chapels, in Manchester, in response to a request for the building of a new chapel. In that communication, they actually queried what had happened to the old chapel:

'Has the old chapel been sold? I cannot understand how otherwise it can have got out of our possession seeing that the lease has fifteen years to run and it would appear that in 1889 on our last renewal the property was used as a school.'

Records show that at a meeting held in 1892, the old chapel was rented out at a cost of £4/0/0, less 2/- [2 shillings] for income tax.

Who actually rented the property is not known; but one can only assume that the old chapel must have gradually fallen into a dilapidated state, since no further evidence of it is to be found.

The surnames of Luke and Stephens appear as leaders of the society that decided, in 1861, to build a new and more substantial chapel. On 10th July 1862, the foundation stone was laid by Mr B.D. Julyan and this was followed with a service in the old Knightor Lane chapel led by Thomas Wenn, one of the circuit ministers. Some of the costs incurred in building the new chapel included the following:-

Clearing the ground	£2/9/0
Cement and concrete	£3/3/3
Plastering	10/0
Copper nails	£2/6/0

The construction was a great building feat, with the owners of horse drawn wagons bringing slate from Delabole quarry; whilst the granite came from the Carn Grey quarries and was supplied free of charge. The Carn Grey Granite Company also provided the stone for the entrance steps at a cost of 6/6 [6 shillings & 6d]. The twenty trustees of the chapel were the first to initiate the necessary funding to start the build. However, in addition, many people from the St Austell area loaned sums of money to assist in meeting the costs.

The names of a number of the original benefactors are inscribed on bricks that form part of the outer wall of the chapel.

On 1st January 1863, the Chapel was opened by the Rev. James Nance from Penzance. On the following Sunday, the opening services continued, with sermons being preached by the Rev. Dr Etheridge in the afternoon and, during the evening, by the Rev. Edwin Blake. The 'collection' taken at this first service was £11/1/9. Seat rents were paid each quarter by the congregation. The deeds of the new chapel were issued on 1st November 1864.

A few years later, in 1867, it was decided to build a Sunday school alongside the new Chapel. Together, these two buildings would provide the religious and social life of the village for many years thereafter. During the weekdays, the Sunday school room was used as a day school for the local children.

Taken from the chapel records of 1900, this is a typical example of the congregation 'collections' at that time:-

Lady Day	£4/5/3
Mid summer	£3/9/3
Michaelmas	£3/17/9
Christmas	£3/19/0

These contributions helped to meet the cost of the general upkeep, repairs and further improvements to the chapel. A new pulpit Bible in 1889 was priced at 14 shillings.

The chapel was enlarged, in February 1904, with the taking down of the end wall to make room for a choir and organ. The extension was marked by rows of bricks being laid by those people who had helped subscribe towards the cost. The new addition was able to fully accommodate the one hundred and fifty strong congregations that would attend at that time. The final cost of £330 was met through subscriptions, public collections, seat rentals and bazaars.

Following completion, the cleaner asked for an increase in her pay as the chapel was now much bigger. It took the committee two weeks to consider this request and they decided that she was to be given £4/10/0 each year. However, for this, she was further required to clean all the windows and extinguish the lights on Sundays.

This photograph taken in the early 1900s shows the chapel dressed for harvest. Note the absence of the organ pipes which were not installed until much later.

In 1921, George Kingdon, who was then living in the USA, visited his old home at Trethurgy and expressed a wish to perpetuate the memory of his late father, Mr James Kingdon, by adding a vestry to the chapel. Tenders for the work were submitted with the contract going to R. Jacobs, at a cost of £535. Mr Kingdon arranged for the ground to be cleared in order for the building work to proceed. Upon completion, the choir and ministers' vestries were presented to the trustees of the chapel in 1922. Again, the cleaner was given an increase in pay to £5/0/0 per annum, due to the extra work involved.

The Kingdon Memorial Vestry.

In 1938, electricity was put in at the chapel. An estimate of £18 was received from 'St Austell Electric Light Company' for the installation work and this was accepted.

Throughout the war years, the congregation continued to hold regular services, so blackouts for the windows had to be put up.

In 1949, a water supply was installed in the Sunday schoolroom. Miss Gunning of *Roseland Cottage* was paid one shilling a year for allowing the pipeline to pass through her garden.

During the 1940s and '50s, the chapel provided the villagers with a calendar of festivals and celebrations. In September of each year, Harvest would be celebrated with two days of festivities taking place. Two services were held on the Sunday - one for the children in the afternoon when they presented their fresh produce gifts and later, an evening service that was enjoyed by all. The chapel would be decorated with pampas grass and colourful ivy and, in pride of place, was the harvest sheaf made by Eustace Bakery. On the Monday, the celebrations continued, with a harvest tea provided by the villagers and this was followed with a service. This final event was held in the Sunday school, where the produce offered in the chapel the previous day was sold. The auctioneer was Mr Mugford and later, Mr Wilfred Keam, with the proceeds of the sale going to the Sunday school.

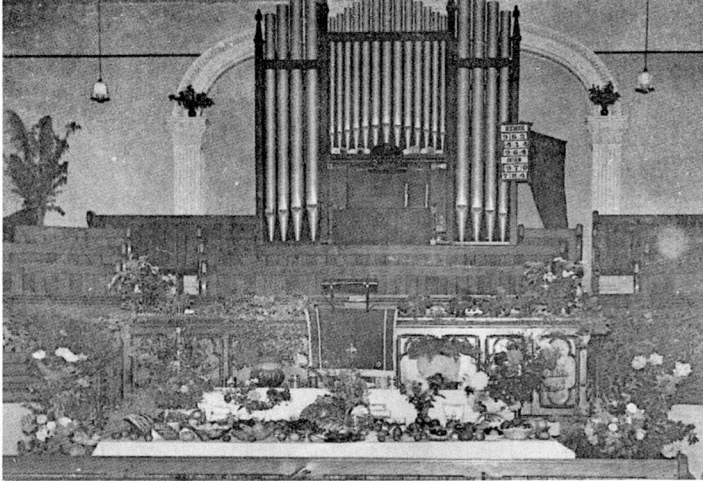

Taken between 1940-'50 with the new organ and pipes in the background.

At Christmas, the children of the village were treated to two parties. One took place at the Sunday school and was funded by Mr Molyneaux of the Lantern China Clay works; whilst the other, held at the village hall, was paid for by the community.

The Easter services were another important event in the annual calendar, when the chapel would be adorned with primroses from the many local hedgerows and displayed in soft beds of moss.

In 1956, Trethurgy Methodist Chapel was specially registered for the solemnisation of marriage, in order that Shirley Kingdon and Michael Wooders could be married there. Their wedding was held on 26 May 1956 and this, was followed with a reception that took place at the Capital Ballroom in St Austell. The happy couple, together with the bridal party, are pictured overleaf.

Left to right: Margaret Crowle, Maureen Manell, Graham Marsh, Michael Wooders, Shirley Kingdon, Sylvia Williams, Rhona Kingdon and Valerie Hicks. In the foreground is Roy Vercoe.

In 1962, the village celebrated the centenary of the chapel. The occasion was marked with a service of thanksgiving on the 26th May. This was conducted by the Rev. Wilfred Wade and was followed by a public tea. The day finished with a centenary rally. The celebrations continued the next day with an afternoon concert by the Bethel Methodist Church Choir and, in the evening, the Rev. Leslie James conducted a service.

Members of the congregation attending the centenary service.

The last marriage service to take place in the chapel was that of Kathryn Keam to Michael Wells from Lostwithiel. Kathryn recalls her happy memories of their wedding in January 1972.

It was a lovely crisp day in January with the chapel looking resplendent in the winter sunshine. The yard had been weeded, the door varnished and the inside sparkled like a new pin. I remember well the minister suggesting that the caretakers and organist will need to be paid, but when I explained the former were my Mum and Dad and the latter, a family friend, he replied with a smile saying "Well, perhaps not then!"

Most of the villagers, then, were known as 'auntie' or 'uncle' regardless of not being blood relatives and many filled the chapel to wish us well. My chauffeur was my cousin in a gleaming white car with ribbons attached and unrecognisable from the normally caked in mud farm vehicle! Everyone had pulled out all the stops to make the day special. My niece, Naomi, and little future brother-in-law, Simon, were wonderful as bridesmaid and page boy.

Being in the building brought back many memories of playing for hours on the moors behind the chapel when we were young and going home just in time for meals. We felt completely safe, outdoors, using our imaginations, and building dens in the bracken. It was a magical place to play. I thought of a previous wedding at the chapel when my friend Elizabeth and I were bridesmaids to Rhona. What an honour that was - we were thrilled! The scent of freesias still reminds me of the bouquets we carried on that wonderful day some fifty odd years ago.

I was christened in the chapel and my Dad often preached there, even though he 'belonged' to the Bodmin circuit. We always knew if mother was in the congregation, even if we were outside, as her singing voice could be heard above all others! As a child, I remember with trepidation having to learn endless recitations or sing solos at the Chapel Anniversary. One year, I decided to do something a little different playing a solo piece on the recorder. I chose the theme from Z Cars, which didn't go down at all well and was deemed 'inappropriate for chapel' - well it was the only tune I could play! Feast day was always most enjoyable with a wonderful spread of yeast and saffron buns and my favourite pink Swiss roll!

My thoughts drifted back to other past times and of characters in the village - 'Aunty' Audrey, the dressmaker, who given some material and sometimes, a pattern, could conjure up whatever outfit was needed. The last one she made me was an outfit, at my request and design, for my cousin's wedding - a psychedelic, multi-coloured hot pants suit. Even though I thought at the time I was the bee's knees, I now cringe at the thought of some outfits I wore in my teens, particularly that one and at a wedding, too!

I remember delivering milk in the pony and trap with Sheldon and joy of joys when we went all the way to St Blazey in the trap to have the horse shod - what a treat! Miss Gunning, [definitely not known as 'auntie' as she was a revered teacher at Fowey Grammar], who lived next door to the chapel, encouraged me to paint and I owe her my lifelong love of art. Major Webb with his goats, Mary & Martha, Aunty Ivy with her beautiful front garden rich with huge pampas grass and Uncle Bill who owned the first television set, whose front room was packed with villagers on FA Cup final day. So many characters came to mind, far too many to mention here, but back in the fifties we knew every person in Trethurgy.

Following the wedding ceremony at the chapel, a reception was held at The Clifden in St Austell and we left for Wiltshire that same evening and where we have since lived for over forty years. Seventeen years after our wedding, we attended a fancy dress party at the local work's club. With the theme being 'shotgun wedding', we dressed as 'bride and groom' in our original attire. We were most pleased to win a substantial cash prize and afterwards the judge said he thought I'd be pleased that I could now remove the cushions from under my dress. I replied, with a smile, that it was impossible as the 'bump' was real and my (first) baby was due in a few weeks!

The chapel, standing proud in the middle of the village, always evokes good memories of my childhood each time I pass. If I listen hard I can still hear Mother singing; Dad in the pulpit; the chapel organ playing and Sheldon shouting to his cows! I've returned to Cornwall many, many times since leaving and always dreamt of returning permanently to my roots. Now I've retired, hopefully, it should soon become a reality.

Kathryn Wells (nee Keam).

Paintings of the Chapel as drawn by Kathryn Wells.

The last funeral service was for Margaret Darlington of Rock Cottage. And the final public service took place on 14th July 1985, when some fifty people from various chapels in the area attended.

Below, is the order of service:

Call to worship	Rev J Knowles Berry
Hymn no. 2	
Opening prayers & Lord's Prayer	R Keam (steward)
Reading - Psalm 27	Rev T Darlington
Hymn no. 52	
Notices & collections	Mrs Pearce (steward)
Reading - Matt 28 1-10	Rev F Bagwell
Hymn no. 1	
Sermon	K Berry
Hymn no. 517	
Prayers	Rev D Forways (Sup Minister)
Hymn no. 672	
Benediction	

During the service, the entries of the first baptism of John Soby in 1838 and the most recent of 1984 were read. In marking the sad demise of the chapel, the service was followed by light refreshments.

After the closure, and on the instructions of the Methodist Circuit, both the Chapel and Sunday school were put up for sale by public auction. This took place at the White Hart Hotel in St Austell on 20th February 1987.

Following their sale, both buildings were converted into private dwellings. The old chapel is presently being used as a holiday let by the current owners. Although the exterior shows little change in appearance, the inside has undergone extensive alterations, yet still retains a number of its original features.

The original windows remain a character feature within the converted building.

The archway that was once above the organ pipes is retained within the main bedroom.

The old solid wooden entrance doors, together with some of the original wood panelling, forms part of the present hallway and galleried sitting room area on the first floor.

Knightor Manor Feast Days

The settlement of *Knightor* is first recorded in 1305, when it was spelt *Creghtyer* meaning 'wrinkled land'. By 1699, Joel Gascoyne's map of Cornwall records it as *Nighter,* with what appears to be two ranges and a tower, indicating a grand building.

By 1805, the Ordnance Survey referred to the settlement as *Nightor* and later, in 1842, the St Austell tithe map records the hamlet as being *Knightor.* At this time, a Walter Robins owned the property, along with much of the surrounding land.

Knightor Manor is the ancient site of this grand house, as was shown by the symbol on the 17th century map. Earlier records showed that in 1305, during the reign of Edward I, it was owned by Robert de Creghtyer. At that time, it formed part of the old manor of Treverbyn, alias *Tre-verbin.* Knightor was to became a seat of the Trevanion family, who also held Gorran Castle. Later, they made nearby Caerhays Castle their seat. Knightor Manor was demolished but re-built again in the nineteenth century.

Although the exact site and style of the original building is not known, many fragments of the original mullioned windows can be found in the existing structure. The current buildings comprise of the old farm-house and out-houses with a date stone of 1623. Other masonry of a similar date is incorporated into the main barn complex. This is a handsome example of a typical late 18th / early 19th century multi-purpose farm building, incorporating both a shippon and threshing barn. It has been extended twice, with both extensions clearly incorporating materials from an earlier building. The date of the extensions broadly coincided with the demolition of the earlier manor house and re-construction of the 19th century farmhouse.

The property has passed through the hands of various owners over the years, including Imerys, the China Clay company, who sold the complex to the present owners. It is now a winery and restaurant.

The Feast Days

Knightor Manor played host to many a Feast Day celebration, which traditionally took place in June. The men, women and children would walk or travel by horse and trap from the nearby villages to attend the celebrations, often singing as they did so. The blue and gold 'Hope and Glory' banner was carried at the front of the procession from the chapel to the Manor house.

On arrival, there would be a great deal of activity taking place and with canvas covered stalls, selling home-made rock, lengths of liquorice and other delicious sweets. The children would spend their money buying the sweets and also, paper trumpets and squeakers.
On these occasions, everyone would dress up in their best clothes.

Notice that the majority, in the photo below, are wearing hats - even the children!   Many of the men and boys would also sport fresh flowers in their buttonholes.

The festivity gave the villagers a chance to meet up with friends and to enjoy a wonderful tea. This would include saffron cake and Cornish clotted cream.

Mr B D Julyan is seated in the middle on the right hand side of the table.

These celebrations would continue until late evening time and, as the folks made their way home, the words of *'Lead kindly Light'* could be heard in the summer breeze.

This newspaper article, published on 20th July 1877, describes a typical feast day of that time.

ST. AUSTELL.

INLAND REVENUE APPOINTMENT.—Mr. William Armstrong, of St. Austell, has been promoted to be officer of Newcastle, 4th Division ; and Mr. C. H. Clark, of Measham, Derby, is to succeed him.

TRETHURGY BAND OF HOPE.—The Trethurgy Band of Hope and Teetotal festival was celebrated on Thursday last. At half-past one o'clock the children and friends met on the school premises, where a procession was formed, headed by the St. Dennis Band, and members bearing flags. The banner, being a new one, was claimed and borne by two of the eldest members, who called themselves the "oldest drunkards reformed." The members proceeded to St. Austell, and returned to Carn Grey Rock, where the children and friends rested themselves awhile, enjoying some select pieces played by the band ; thence to a nice field, kindly lent by a friend, where at four o'clock the children had their treat of tea, cake, &c. At five o'clock there was a public tea, largely and respectably attended. At seven o'clock a public meeting was held in the chapel. Mr. Chas Rundle presided, and ably addressed the meeting, after which addresses were delivered by the Rev. W. H. Weatherhill, of Par ; Mr. N. Nettle, of Tywardreath ; Mr. Buzza, of St. Austell ; Mr. Curton, of St. Austell ; and Mr. S. Dyer, of Bugle. Pieces were sung by the choir, and there were recitations and dialogues by the children and friends. The tea tables were presided over by Mrs. Nancollas, Mrs. Bassett, Mrs. Coon, Miss Dyer, Miss Floyd, and Miss Lucas. The weather was all that could be desired, and the proceedings passed off successfully. This society has made rapid progress ; it was established last February, and already has considerably more than one hundred members of both the young and aged.

After an absence, the feast day was revived in 1972, with the music being provided by the St Dennis Band. This special occasion continued to take place in the village right up until the closure of the chapel. The celebrations are still much remembered for the saffron buns served at tea-time and the maypole dancing that preceded it.

School Life in Trethurgy

On 15th January 1873, the village school opened its doors to being a day school with 16 pupils. The accommodation was divided into separate boys and girls school rooms and able to accommodate 167 children.

Below is a photograph of the pupils at Trethurgy Board School in 1897. On the left, are the pupil teachers: Rose Nicholls and Emmy Julian and, on the right: Miss Bassett, the class teacher.

This photo is reproduced by courtesy of Valerie Jacob (nee Mugford).

During the early 1900s, those children who lived too far away to go home for their dinners were provided with a meal by Libby-Ann, who lived in the village. The parents would provide her with the ingredients to make the dinners, with pasties always a favourite!

The following are some of the entries taken from the school log book:

1875: 19 July   - 112 children are on roll
      13 Sept.   - Some of the children who have been absent for harvest week returned this week.
1876: 11 June   - Holiday on Wednesday afternoon due to Camborne Show and Fair.
1877: 30 July   - Punished three girls for playing truant.
1878: 23 Sept.   - John Harris died on Monday morning from bronchitis. Fresh cases of fever.

1878: 12 Nov.   - The weather is cold and snow is on the ground. The snow storms were severe in the afternoon.

1879: January   - Sarah Paul commenced duties. 81 present.

17 Jan.   - Susan Ball died on Thursday from fever.

21 March   - Attendance improved in the infant department. Called on Mrs Carter and spoke to her about her two daughters' disobedience in school hours.

1880: 02 Jan.   - Find it hard to work with any pleasure, the attendance is improving consequently the rooms are crammed. The Infants schoolroom cannot be used as stove will not work. I have been forced to send the children to the playground in order to air the rooms every morning.

20-24 Sept.   - Holiday on Thursday for the Sunday school Centenary. Got a list of children who had left since November 1779 for Mr Gill. [*This would have included attendance at the old chapel in Knightor Lane*]

1881: 09-13 Feb.   - Laura Thomas from the 4th class died on Wednesday. Have called the children in at 1.30 so that they may be out in time to attend her funeral. Received drawing certificates. Taught the children a new song 'Far Away.'

08-12 Mar.   - Having to pass through the lobby, the children bring the plaster in on their feet. Consequently, the classrooms and schoolroom have a coat of plaster on them. While the plaster was taken down, everything and everybody were covered with a coating of plaster dust. The children are more or less masons as it is impossible to keep them out of the mortar and dust.

15-19 Mar.   - The average number of pupils for the week is 92.

22 March   - Attendance very low this week, although the weather has been fine. The children have been kept home to till potatoes and to pick up stones. I have got a list of the absentees for the attendance officer.

07 May   - Holiday on Monday (Whitsuntide). Very small school. Fair on Tuesday and many of the children stayed at home to go the fair.

23-27 Aug.   - Miss Tyack's lesson on 'Thrift' was an improvement on her last. Gave the pupil teachers an examination in Geography during Thursday dinner hour. The results were fair.

20-24 Sept.   - School still small. A large number are sick with measles in the infants and many older girls are kept at home to nurse the little ones.

1882: 03 March   - Small school. Very wet day and a number of children are at home with swollen throats. Olivia Bastion died last Friday with an ulcerated throat.

1882: 19 May	- Lillian Harvey died from the Infants room. Emily Harvey at home for three days.
23 June	- Sent to Attendance Officer a list of children who have left school and gone to work under age.
11 August	- Sent out 33 bills for school fees.
18 August	- Issued 18 summonses for arrears of school fees.
1883: 18 May	- Holiday Monday and Tuesday because of Whit Monday and Fair Day. Very small school this week with average of 75. No fresh cases of fever.
1884: 29 Sept.	- The children came at 1pm instead of 2-o-clock and were dismissed an hour earlier as a great number of them wanted to attend a tea treat.
1890: 01 Oct.	- Two fresh cases of scarlet fever in the village. The School Board closed the school due to measles and scarlet fever.
14 Nov.	- The Infant boys are learning to sew. Several older girls are doing their knitting and have commenced samplers.

Example of a sampler as sewn by the girls at the school - Courtesy of Brian Jacob.
The original is to be found in the St Austell Museum at the Market House.

1892: 11 Jan.	- School closed because of another fall of snow.
1893: 17 Oct.	- 107 children present.
1897: 21 May	- 39 children absent. Most of them absent because they went to see a wedding. A half day holiday was given because of a cricket match in the village.

1898: 18 June	- 128 out of 158 present.
29 Aug.	- Jane Abraham has left school being over 13 to assist mother at home with the younger children.
1904: 24 May	- Opened school this morning after Whitsuntide holiday. Registers not marked as only a few children present owing to bad weather.
27 May	- Closed for Feast Day.

Inspection Report 1904

Visited this school. Better cloakroom and lavatory accommodation is badly needed. Most of the desks are too high and too far from the seats.
The discipline of school is satisfactory and the work not without merit in some respects but more should be done to develop children's intelligence.
There is a need to develop the power of expression both in speech and writing.

1906: 01 Dec.	- Attendance very low - 51% due to bad weather. 52 children on roll.
1907: 18 Oct.	- Opened school at 9am. 5 children only present due to the bad weather.
1908: 31 Aug.	- Opened school after summer holiday - 47 children present.
15 Sept.	- 40 girls were taken to the Polytechnic exhibition at Camborne.
09 Oct.	- Average attendance for past week is 43 with 45 on books. School closed in the afternoon for an attendance holiday.
1909: 03 March	- Opened school this morning. The weather was rough. Only 14 children were present. I dismissed them and closed the school for the afternoon.
29 April	- Opened school at 1.15 this afternoon and dismissed the school at twenty to four, there being a carnival.
04 June	- Teresa Williams died on Thursday.
02 July	- Beatrice Kelly has left school being over 14.
1910: 19 April	- The school will be closed tomorrow for the late King's funeral. *(King Edward VII)*
15 July	- Several children absent this week due to haymaking.
1911: 26 Jan.	- Two lessons - drill and singing - were omitted today because the mistress has lost her voice.

Taken outside the chapel in 1910 - In the back row, second from right, is Ivy Crowle (nee Julian) and in the front, third from right, is Stan Tregidga.

Inspection Report 1912

The school has made no perceptible advance during the last two years. The dull and lifeless teaching is reflected in the mental attitude of the children. The inadequate lavatory arrangements have been previously pointed out. There is limited unsuitably arranged cloakroom accommodation - the pegs are too close together. The slate in the boys' office (toilets) appears to be in a dangerous condition.

1913: 03 March - Miss L Pascoe appointed.
      11 March - Wilfred Wellington stood on a window sill and accidently broke a window pane.
1914: 04 Dec.   - A very rough and stormy morning only 16 children present out of 33.
1915: 11 Oct.   - The schoolroom will be required for the Harvest Tea. Afternoon session will start thirty minutes earlier and the end of the day will finish thirty minutes earlier.
1920: 15 June - Teacher and children took a nature walk and a visit to a clay works from 3.35 to 4.15. [*Probably, the Lantern China Clay Works at Hennals Lane*]

1925: 07 Dec.	- The caretaker was unable to light the stove today owing to the beams catching on fire on the previous Friday. A fire has been lit in the grate. Not a success - the room is full of smoke.
1926: 20 Oct.	- New coal box from Hawkes [*St Austell Ironmonger*] £8/6.
1927: 04 July	- Very wet, stormy morning. 14 children present out of 32.
23 Nov.	- Example of a punishment letter:-

I am sorry I threw stones on the school premises and I promise not to do so again.   Michelle Dewings, Edmund Church and George Jones

1928: 07 March	- Number on roll is 26.

School Life during the War

The Village Hall was used as the school during the war years. On 9th October 1940, it opened as a school for all the evacuees who were billeted in the village and surrounding area.

Miss Moody was put in charge of the morning sessions that would take place from 9:00a.m until mid-day. The afternoon sessions started at 2:00p.m and ended at 4:30p.m. The first day of opening saw 16 of the 20 children who had been evacuated from the

Tottenham area of London, being present; also, 2 from Woodford, 2 from Acton and 2 local children, making a total of 22 in all.

The following extracts are taken from the log book of the war years.

1940: 14 Oct.   - 12 Cornish children were admitted making a total of 35. All children were requested to carry gas masks.

     20 Nov.   - Two air raids alerts today during the morning. All children were in school today.

Between 18 Nov. 1940 and 06 Jan. 1941 - Thirteen air raid alerts lasting on average of two hours took place.

1941: 28 Jan.   - Called upon Mr Webb today, our air raid warden, about fire watching. Mr Webb is willing to be around premises during alerts.

     21 April   - Today 11 children from Bristol were admitted and 2 from Carclaze which brings the number on roll to 41.

     23 April   - 2 more children from Bristol were admitted today.

     12 May   - 5 children from Plymouth were admitted today. Total on roll now stands at 48.

     06 June   - Red Cross Flag Day. £6/3 collected and sent to Mrs Luke.

1942: 07 Aug.   - Air raid alert at 2.10. The all clear was given at 2.30.

     28 Oct.   - Air raid alert at 1.20. The all clear was given at 1.40.

1943: 18 Jan.   - Air raid alert at 1.10. The all clear was given at 1.30.

     02 March   - Air raid alert at 2.50. The all clear was given at 3.05.

     12 March   - Air raid alert at 1.25. The all clear was given at 1.40.

     24 March   - In celebration of Empire Day, an Empire Service was held in the morning. Sports were held in the afternoon. These were held in the hall due to inclement weather. A prize for the child winning the highest points was presented with a prize by Mrs Ford.

     24 June   - Air raid alert at 10.30 this morning. It lasted until 10.50.

     28 June   - The school went on a nature walk to Carn Gray Rock. The children saw people at work in the hay field and picked whortle berries.

     05 July   - The school went for a nature walk to Hennals. Thirty seven kinds of wild flowers were gathered.

     19 Nov.   - Air raid alert.

     10 Dec.   - The children were given a talk on *'butterfly'* bombs.

[The *'butterfly'* bomb was so named because, once deployed, it gave the appearance of a large butterfly. It was one of the first cluster bombs used.]

1944: 12 May   - The school is closing today and children being transferred to Carclaze and Boscoppa on Monday.   *H. Mitchell*

Marjorie Sampson [nee Bennetts], who lived in the village, recalls a memory of her brothers, Michael and Aubrey. Both attended the school and on one occasion, in the early 1940s, their dog 'Peter' sat outside the school all day long until the children were dismissed in the afternoon.

Although the day school was transferred to the village hall in 1940, parties and concerts continued to take place in the old school-room. Mr and Mrs Body were responsible for keeping the Sunday school going during the 1960/70s. The Sunday school sessions continued to take place there until the chapel was closed in 1985.

Above are the children who took part in the 1971 nativity play.
Mary was played by Louise Harvey and Joseph by Mark Seward.
Rachel Seward, Rachel Body and Donna Thorn are three of the angels
with Andrew Trudgeon and Chris Grace, being two of the wise men.
In the back row, second from left, is Jackie Trudgeon.

The Village Institute / Hall

The inspiration behind the building of the hall came from the Duke of Windsor - the then, Duke of Cornwall, and patron of the British Legion. At a time of high unemployment in Cornwall, the British Legion was urging its members to come forward and involve themselves within the local communities. A committee was formed in 1933, under the chairmanship of Mr W.C. Hicks, and resulted in a stone laying ceremony taking place in March 1934.

With the unemployed volunteer workforce making an enthusiastic start to the project, it was hoped that the building would be completed within twelve months. However, it was to take three years longer for the very best of reasons. Employment within the china clay industry had picked up and this resulted in the building work slowing down.

Pictured at the laying of the foundation stones in 1934 are the benefactors of the hall. These include: Eddy Jones, Arthur Trevains, R.H. Luke, Claude Selleck, Fred Ede, Rev. C.F. Jones - Vicar of Luxulyan, Wilce Mugford, Richard Kingdon & J. Brewer. The young girl at the front is Joan Mugford.

Many of the donors involved in the building have their names inscribed on individual stones within the walls of the hall. These are still clearly evident and a reminder of the institute's beginning. All the blocks used in the build were made voluntarily; with only the roof and the rendering being done professionally. Mains electricity was also installed at the time of construction. It cost the sum of £791/8/5 to complete the project, but when the building was officially opened, a shortfall of £222 still remained to be found.

The grand opening took place on the 1st July 1937. From the steps of the hall, Rev. C.F. Jones – the Vicar of Luxulyan, offered prayers and the vice-chairman, Mr R.H. Luke, conveyed details of how the scheme had originated and progressed to completion. The Chairman, Mr W.C. Hicks, then called upon Major Sassoon to open the hall; but firstly, asked Betty Wilton, whose father had done much of the woodwork, to present a 'silver key' to Major Sassoon.

Major Sassoon – the Manager of Selleck Nicholls stands in the centre.
On the left are: R.H Luke, A. Trevains and W.C. Hicks, and to the right: Claude Sellick, Rev. C.F. Jones and J. Brewer.
The young girl is Betty Wilton.

The celebration that was to follow marked the end of three years of tremendous community spirit and endeavour. The villagers celebrated the opening by listening to the St Dennis Silver Band playing outside the hall and later, enjoyed a sumptuous high tea outside the school room. The celebrations continued in the evening, with a concert by the St Dennis children's choir. One much looked forward to acquisition within the new building was a billiard table to provide a recreational facility. The hall also provided a stage, meeting rooms and other leisure equipment for the villagers.

For many years afterwards, along with the chapel, the hall became the centre of the social life of the village community.

During the war, the American servicemen, who were based in the grounds of *Tregrehan House,* would use Trethurgy village hall for Saturday evening dances. The village would hear sounds that were so different to their ears, as the soldiers brought along their own style of dancing and music. The 'Lindy' was a mixture of many dance styles and based on jazz, tap, breakaway and the Charleston.

The black American soldiers were not allowed to attend these dances. They were segregated from the white soldiers in a completely different camp at Greensplat, west of Carthew.

As previously mentioned, the institute was also used as the school during the war years, although we have not discovered the reason why this was so!

When the war ended, the hall became less frequently used and, as a result, the building got somewhat neglected. However, due to its original sound construction, it managed to withstand those years of neglect.

The Village Hall 1976 - 1985

In June 1976, an open meeting took place to discuss the future of the hall. The options put forward included the possibility of selling the hall, with the monies going to the charity commissioners; or to continue to keep it open for the future benefit of the village. It was unanimously decided on the latter, under the appointment of a new management committee. Making greater use of the hall was imperative and a number of proposed suggestions were discussed. As a result, Terry Minear was to organise and run a weekly youth club, with children from outside of the village also being invited to come along. Two weeks after its inception, it had a membership of some fourteen juniors and thirty-six seniors. Throughout the seventies, the hall was further used by a number of organisations and for different purposes, from private parties to courses and meetings of all kind. The committee worked extremely hard to raise money and provide the villagers with a calendar of events. The bonfire night displays and pasty supper that followed were very popular; as were the children's Christmas parties and carol services. Organised barn dances also enjoyed much success and popularity.

A particularly special time was the 'Queen's Silver Jubilee' in June 1977. Two hundred flags were ordered for the event and plans put in place for a series of celebrations. Two of the organised activities were a fancy dress football match and a disco; both by Terry Minear. Mrs Crowle was invited to present the children of the village with Jubilee coins.

Further improvements to the original hall took place in 1979, with the construction of a new toilet block and a new roof in 1988. This ensured that the whole community was able to continue to enjoy the facility and activities provided. Again, a variety of fund-raising events were arranged to help to meet the cost of the projects, from coffee evenings and bazaars to sponsored walks. The villagers also, from time to time, ran a stall at Par market.

Over the years, the appointed committees have striven to find ways of keeping the hall going - both financially and in providing a varied range of social activities for the community to partake in and enjoy. One such example was a sponsored walk that was held in August 1985 and raised £250; whilst others, included organised coach trips to different places in Devon and Cornwall and also, some boat trips. What has been clearly apparent over the years is the immense enthusiasm shown to keep the community 'feel' of the village going.

As well as maintaining and improving the facilities and fabric of the village hall, trees were planted around the playing field. Furthermore, the addition of improved drainage and erection of goal posts have taken place.

The chairman of the committee from 1985 to 2012 was Lloyd Rowett and it was he, who was responsible for many of the improvements that were carried out to the hall; such as the new flooring, insulation of the walls and the added provisions for disabled people. Also, in obtaining the necessary grants for these improvements to take place. Mr Rowett's valued endeavours will never be forgotten! Prior to this, previous chairman were Mr Mugford, Mr Cross, Mr Darlington and Mr Tynan. The present chairman, Matthew Luke, took over in 2013.

The outside area of the hall has also been enhanced over the years. The front borders were prepared and planted in the early 1990s with money that was left to the village hall by the late Mr Jack Luke.

The triangular piece of land with the signpost has also been well maintained over the years. Sandy Foord and her father were often to be found tending this ground. The garden was made in memory of Sylvia Trudgeon, who was both very popular and actively involved.

Frank Johns also spent many an hour keeping the outside areas of the hall in good order. He and his wheelbarrow were a common sight, as were his colourful and humorous hats!

A ninetieth birthday tea party was arranged in Frank's honour in 1996. He was so well thought of that a commemorative plaque was placed in the wall in recognition of all his hard work.

Above, Frank is pictured with Terry Watts alongside the plaque.

A strong community spirit has prevailed in Trethurgy over many years with village events, such as the annual flower show, always being well supported.

This picture shows an exhibition of flowers, fruit, vegetables and cookery that took place in 1985. The individual winners: Mr W. Keam, Mrs E. Grace, Mrs V. Chapman, Mrs Keam, Miss B. Denslow, Mrs M. Seward, Miss L. Wooders and Mr E. Hore were presented with their prizes by the Rev. Brian Spencer.

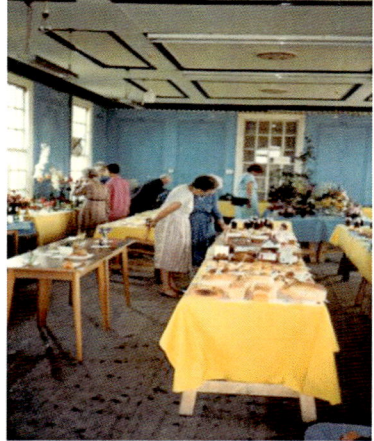

Below, in the re-decorated hall, some of the villagers are enjoying a cream tea during an organised 'garden safari'. Five local gardens were opened up to the public and the monies collected again helped boost the village funds.

On this occasion, Sylvia and Peter Moyle, Marian and Mick Johnson, Ann and Dave Jeffs, Diana Martin and Sandy Foord were the volunteers who put their lovely gardens on show.

The Playing Field

The playing field was created in the late 1960s from some previously rough ground. It was owned by ECC (later, Imerys) and had been often covered in china clay waste. The project demanded much hard work with the local folk again banding together to form working parties to clear the undergrowth.

In May 1998, a special ceremony was held to celebrate the handing over of the Trethurgy Playing Field deeds. Dr Gronno is pictured making the official opening and handing over the deeds to Sandy Foord.

Afterwards, the villagers enjoyed a celebratory tea in the hall with a specially made cake that depicted the football pitch on the field.

On another occasion, the villagers enjoy the music of the 'All Stars' band during a village fete. The hall was set up with refreshments and an *'It's a knockout'* competition took place on the playing field.

The 'All Stars' band often played at these village events, with Peter Minear organising the band and drawing in musicians from the local area.

Amongst other popular events to take place in the village were the annual Christmas Carol singing; 'Sports fun days' and 'Parties in the Park', as well as the special commemorative celebrations.

A *Sports fun day activity taking place in August 1993.*

The carol singers would tour around the village and afterwards, continue their singing in the hall with mulled wine and mince pies being served.

Katherine Wright and Avril Moyle, together with some friends, organised the 'Party in the Park' event for a number of years.

The 'Queen's Golden Jubilee' tea party was held in the playing field in June 2002. There were lots of games and sports arranged for the children to enjoy and medals were presented at the end of the day. This was another example of a well organised and attended community project that brought the villagers together to share in a memorable occasion.

Village Life

Trethurgy village has seen a few modest developments since the 1960s. More traffic on the local roads in recent years has been a noticeable feature and it is hard to imagine that any farmer would, nowadays, take a herd of cattle along those roads.

Taken in 1965, Mr Croucher's cows, after grazing in the background meadow that is now 'Knightor Close', make their daily walk through the village to his 'Carn Grey Farm' for milking.

Harold Hambly, the local milkman from 'Hills Farm', is seen turning a field of hay during the summer of 1965. In the background, on the left, is the village hall; whilst the stack of Alseveor clay dry is to the right.

This farm sale in 1967 at *Carn Grey* - later, to be known as *Trelawney* - attracted many people. The sand tip and workings, as shown to the left of the picture, is now the home of 'The Eden Project' at Bodelva. If you look closely in the centre, you will observe the Garker Clay Dry.

Below, the Bodelva tip again dominates the background. To the left of it, the workings at the end of *Hennals Lane* form part of the 1960's landscape; whilst some horses grazing in the field at *Carn Grey* appear in the foreground.

The picture below shows the village in 1968. *Bay View* is on the right and, to the left: *Chytan Farm* and *Chytan Cottage*. *Bay View* was built in the 1880s by Mr B.D. Julyan.

Trethurgy once had a flourishing shop and post office which is sadly missed today; not only for its commercial use, but as a hub for the villagers to meet and pass the time of day. The stone building below: to the right of the two trees, is the old village shop in the grounds of *Rockhurst*.

In 1966, the old shop was demolished and a new one built adjoining *Rockhurst*. A temporary shop operated in the flat-roofed building whilst the construction took place. Eric Martin's cows are seen grazing in the field where *The Friary* now stands.

Trethurgy post office closed its door for the final time on 27th August 1987. The last post mistress, Margaret Mugford, was in charge for ten years. Prior to this, the post office was run from the 1950s by Kath Davidson.

This photo was taken on the last day of trading of the Post Office.

Taken in 1967, *Rose Cottage* is shown to the right and looks across towards *Rock Cottage* and *Belle View.*

The field between these houses and the road is where the small estate of *Knightor Close* now stands. It was built in that same year by Jim Cory, a well known Cornish builder.

The entrance to 'Knightor Close' with 'Rock Cottage' in the background.

Old Houses of the Village

These maps show Trethurgy with the buildings as were present in 1881.

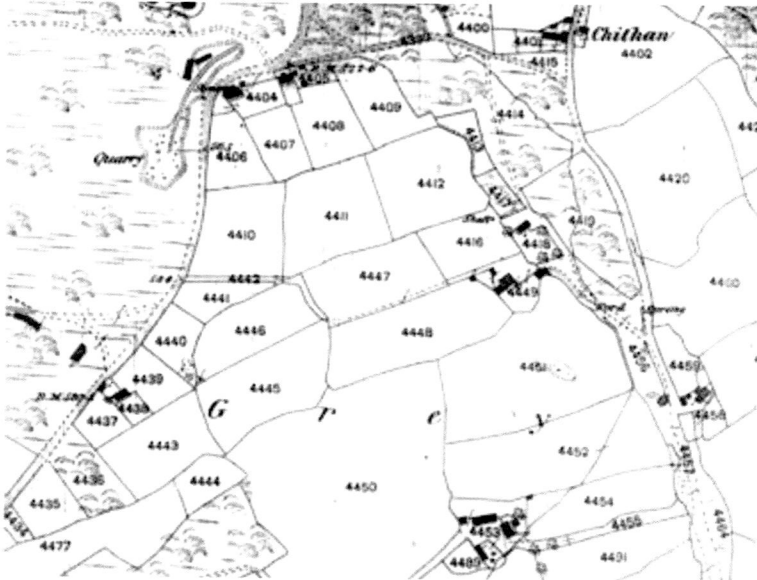

In the centre of the village is, reportedly, the oldest house. Nowadays, known as *The Cottage,* it was once used as a *'kiddlewink'* or drinking house and licensed to sell beer or cider. However, illegally smuggled brandy, rum and gin were also available to regular customers.

The name *kiddlewink* comes from the words *'kiddle'* - this being a smuggled liquor and *'wink'* - a gesture made to the bartender to acquire that drink!

Although now a single residential property, prior to the 1940s, it was two separate cottages. One of the original Tudor period chimneys still remains in place.

Most of the older houses of the village were built in the mid-nineteenth century and leased from the Treverbyn manor. The majority were used as miners' cottages.

A typical example of such a property is that of *Roseland* which is located in *Chapel Lane* and appears overleaf. Although there is no evidence of it on the early maps we have accessed, it is thought to have been built around 1850. In 1906, Ellen Tregidga took out a 100-year lease on this house for an annual rent of £1 and continued to live there until her death in 1941. In 1961, it was sold as a freehold property to Doris Gunning for the sum of £117.

This 1906 map shows Roseland alongside the chapel and Sunday school.

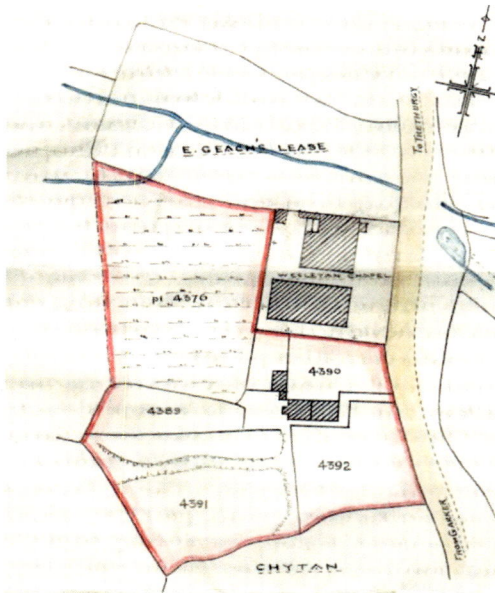

Little Grey Cottage is about 200 years old and again, was built as a tin miner's cottage. The miner was employed at the Garker Valley tin mine. Originally, it had one room upstairs and one down. However, it has been extended over the years and is now a large four-bedroomed house. It is being run as a successful 'bed and breakfast' business by the owners, Marian and Mick Johnson.

Little Grey Cottage in 2010.

These three cottages of the early 1900s are beside a track that leads to the old clay works and farm at Alseveor. Bertram Mugford is pictured in the foreground, alongside three friends.

The same cottages in the 1960s.

They were converted into a single cottage in the 1990s and have recently, undergone further renovation work. It is now *Restormel Cottage* and appears as below.

This is *Butts Cottage* as it was during the 1960s. Originally, the left side of the building was a stable with a barn above it; and the right side was the dairy. The Kingdon family once operated a haulage business from here.

The modernised 'Butts Cottage' in 2013.

Rose Cottage was built in 1845, originally as two small cottages providing one-up and one-down accommodation. This was to house miners who were working in the area at the peak of the mining industry.

Later, around 1885, an extension was built on the front and linked to the original cottages to make it into a single four-bedroomed dwelling. The 'pebbledash' finish that we see in the picture was done in 1910 and retained until 1959, when further restoration was undertaken.

The lease on *Rose Cottage,* along with some additional land, was purchased from the Treverbyn Estates in 1962, with some 49 years remaining to run. A flat roof extension was later built in 1965, in accordance with the planning regulations of that time. Additional alterations have since been carried out, with the present day building now revealing the original granite stonework.

This is all that remains of a window of the wash-house that was once attached to *Moorland House*. Through this window, the quarry workers would be paid their wages by Miss Nicholls, who was a member of the Sellick Nicholls family that owned the quarry. This process of payment was done right up to the time of the quarry closing in 1939.

Nearby, was once situated a tap from which the villagers would draw water, although it is no longer there. However, what does still remain at the top of *Chapel Lane* is part of an original fireplace from the old cottage that once stood there.

Hennals Lane

Hennals Lane which is off *Chapel Lane* lead to the Lantern China Clay works that was opened in the early twentieth century and closed in 1955. The name *'Hennals'* begs the question: *"Why that name?"* One possible answer lies in the name of a field that was found on the tithe map of 1842. The field was numbered 4436 and occupied by a Richard Julian. It was described as being rough pasture and called *'Henowls moor'*.

Hennals Lane is also recalled as being the home to a number of gypsy families who lived both sides of the river. Their homes were tents, nestled between the trees and the undergrowth. The wood smoke from the camp fires would fill the air and the sound of their 'chatter' often echoed up to the village.

The gypsies worked on the local farms throughout the year and would further supplement their income by making clothes pegs, as shown opposite. Using fashioned hazel-wood twigs, the peg was fastened by a nail and bound with strips of metal taken from used 'corn beef' tins. They also made delicate wooden flowers which they dipped into paint and shaped like chrysanthemums. Another of their money making ventures would be collecting scrap metal.

Phoebe Bull was another local gypsy who lived in Trethurgy. She, however, lived alone in a small gypsy caravan on some land opposite to *Bay View*. Phoebe worked as a cleaner for the Luke family at *Menear Farm* and is remembered for always wearing an apron over her clothes.

Walking down *Hennals Lane* - a few yards from the gate, you will find amongst the undergrowth a hole that is most definitely man made. It is believed that dynamite was stored here for use at the Lantern China Clay works which was sited at the far end of the lane.

Further along the path and opening up into a 'clearing' [bottom left] was once the site of a sand tip. The fishing lake [bottom right], although very pretty, is extremely deep and out of bounds to the public. This peaceful spot was once the clay pit of this area. Nearby, but now derelict, are the ruined offices of the Lantern china clay works.

The Local Landscape

This landscape in 2014 looks very different to that of the early 1900s when Trethurgy was an industrial mining and quarrying area.

Below is 'The Plant' as it appeared in 1912, when the quarry was at the peak of its production. This stone plant was sited just below the entrance to the bottom quarry. In front of the left hand building can be seen the chimney of a static steam engine. This would have provided the power to the stone crusher.

THE PLANT, TRETHURGY

The granite was used for headstones, lintels and building stones. All the left over chippings would be graded and sorted out for use in road construction.

Parts of a railway system that linked the top and bottom quarries can still be seen near to the top quarry, where the granite would then have been transported by road. Selleck Nicholls owned and worked both of the quarries. The bottom one closed in 1931 but the top quarry continued in production until the outbreak of the Second World War. Most of the workforce then left, either to fight in the war or work in other Cornish quarries.

The horse and trap, in the foreground of the previous picture, is on the road close to *Carn Grey Cottage*. A story is told that on one summer day occasion, a baby named Billy Trevains, who lived in that house with his parents, was in his pram in the garden when the quarry opposite was blasting the rock. To his mother's horror, a stone hurtled into his pram and narrowly missed the unsuspecting baby. This near tragic occurrence was partly responsible for the closure of the bottom quarry.

These towers are all that remains of the plant at the top quarry.

Another story told is of Ray Hamley, who, for many years, had cycled from his home in St Blazey to work in the quarry at Trethurgy. He then got married and bought a house in *Butts Lane*, just before the outbreak of the war. When, as was previously mentioned, the war stopped production in the quarry, Ray had to seek work elsewhere. He happened to find a job down at Par Docks; which meant that poor Ray had to get on his bike, once again, to get to and from his new workplace!

Taken from close to the bottom quarry - at the site of the old plant, this photo shows how the village looked in 1964. *Rockhurst* is in the centre and behind it, is a small granite building. This was the shop and post office.

Above, we see a wider aspect picture of the village in 1964. To the right are the chapel and school. This view looks towards the bottom quarry and, in the centre where the chimney stack stands, is now the playing field.

It is of interest to compare this outlook with that of the present day landscape [see p56] to become aware of the extent of development that has taken place during the past fifty years.

The bottom quarry as it is seen today.

The photograph below was taken in the early 1900s from the site of the present village hall and looks across towards *Rockhurst*. The small building, on the opposite side of the road to *Rockhurst,* is that of the shop which was owned by Mr Wellington. He would often be seen with his horse and trap in delivering the groceries.

Although his shop was in Trethurgy, Mr Wellington lived in *Restineas Cottage* in Garker. Close to the old shop was a water shute which provided the villagers with their clean, fresh water. Mr Tom Ford recalls when, as a pupil at the school, it was his daily task to fetch the water for the pupils. The shute fulfilled the daily needs of the villagers up until the 1920s, when a mains water supply was put in.

Taken in 1902 from the higher ground of the present playing field and looking towards the top of the village, the photo shows *Ruby Cottage* in the foreground. It was once the 'count house' for the iron industry in this area. Attached to the cottage is a building that was once the 'drying house' where the miners' clothes would be dried. On the right hand side, opposite to *Ruby Cottage,* can be seen two little goat houses. The field above the cottage is now the site of *Knightor Close* and occupied by ten bungalows.

This is actually a copy of a postcard that was sent by Miss Selleck in 1903 to show her new home. It is marked with a 'cross' in the top right hand corner and now named *Moorland House*.

If you look very carefully, you will just about see what appears to be the gable end of the original chapel of 1817. It is slightly right of the house at the top left hand corner of the picture!

Excavations at Trethurgy Round

Although Trethurgy is a small hamlet with once only a handful of dwellings within its quiet, peaceful community, a rather startling discovery took place in the early 1970s that was to provide sensational media coverage in the local and national papers, as well as on the television news programmes.

Quite unknown to many a generation who had lived in Trethurgy, evidence was to be found of Cornish homes from the second century laying buried beneath the surface of a small field on the outskirts of the village. It was a member of the Cornish Archaeological Society - Mr Peter Shepherd from Gorran, who was responsible for this discovery. Whilst looking through some papers, he had noticed a reference on a 19th century tithe map to a *'Round Field'* at Trethurgy. A small dig was initially conducted and it was confirmed as being the site of an ancient 'round'.

This was in 1972 and, with one of the English China Clays (ECC) sand tips moving rapidly in the direction of the site, the company kindly agreed to temporarily suspend their tipping schedule. Consequently, in 1973, some sixty diggers moved into the area, with some coming from as far away as America.

These photographs of 1973 show the remains of some of the ancient dwellings.

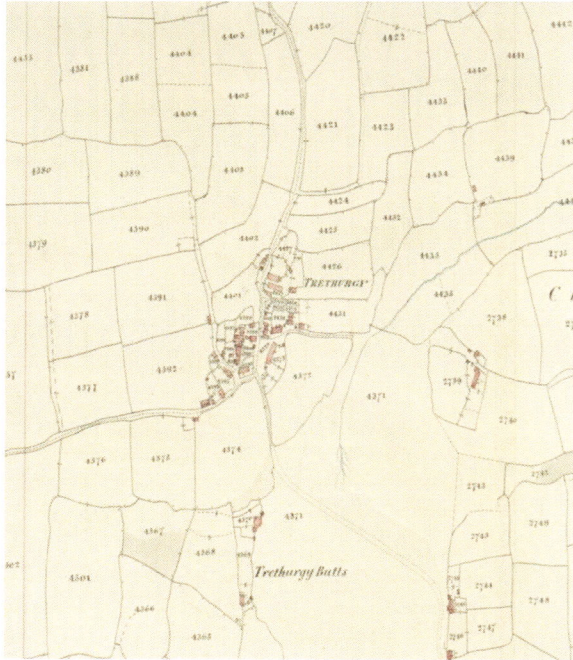

The site of the 'Round' can be seen in 4366 - left of 'Trethurgy Butts'.
[Reference: TM/8 - Courtesy of Cornwall Record Office]

*An aerial photograph, taken in September 1973, from the north
and showing the hill slope position of the 'Round'.*
[Reproduced by permission of Royal Naval Air Station, Culdrose]

Of some two hundred 'rounds' in Cornwall, this was the only one that has been completely excavated and proved conclusively that it was occupied from 200 to 600 AD. Henrietta Miles [now Quinnell] - a tutor in archaeology at Exeter University at that time - described the dig as "Almost certainly the most important archaeological dig ever made in Cornwall." She went on to say that the hill top settlement was built by Cornish Celtic people while part of the Roman Empire.

The settlement was surrounded by a massive oval shaped fortification between six and ten feet high and some ten feet wide, with a deep dry outer ditch to keep out potential marauders. The barricade was faced on both sides with stone walls. Pebbles found nearby might have provided ammunition for sling warfare.

Remains of some eight huts were found within the settlement and, although in ruins, it was possible to discover that they had low walls with thatched roofs. The centre of the settlement was a large cobbled yard with the huts and lean-to buildings around the outside. It was estimated that at the height of its prosperity, the 'round' would have had eighty residents, mainly engaged in agriculture.

The dig revealed a number of exciting finds, including a 'saddle quern' - a granite dish in which corn was pounded. Also, the remains of bowls made from Elvan stone. Fragments of pots that were found indicated that the inhabitants had contacts not only with places in England, but as far away as the Eastern Mediterranean. One of the most important cargoes was wine from the Mediterranean which must have arrived in very large pots, since more than forty fragments had been found.

At the entrance to the site could be seen huge granite slabs over which chariots would have travelled. Also, scratch marks that had been created by the opening and closing of a set of entrance gates. Blackened stones in the huts further revealed the situation of the fireplace. It was thought that, eventually, the inhabitants of the settlement had drifted away rather than something catastrophic affecting the community.

Sadly, the site has since been covered by china clay waste and no visible evidence of it remains.

For full report details, refer to the publication 'Excavations at Trethurgy Round, St Austell: Community and Status in Roman and Post-Roman Cornwall by Henrietta Quinnell [ISBN 1-903798-12-4]

Clay Works, Quarries and Mines by W B Shipley

The Tithe Maps and their accompanying survey books, known as apportionments, were drawn up under the 'Tithe Commutation Act of 1836', which substituted payments in kind to payments in cash. They could be used to provide a snapshot of land ownership, occupation and land use in a parish or town in the 19th century. An examination of the 1842 tithe map of the parish of St. Austell reveals a total of 11 clay works and 8 mines. However, a close look at and around Trethurgy on this map reveals no evidence of any industrial activity, with the exception of a blacksmith's shop at the top of the village where _Moorland House_ now stands. The nearest mine was situated at Carclaze.

A study of the Ordnance survey map of 1882, however, shows the Wheal Ruby and Treverbyn iron mines, although being disused at this time. Also, the clay pits at Pentruff and Alseveor, together with their attendant settling tanks and drying sheds [clay dries]. The two quarries at Carn Grey are also shown. So, it would appear, in a space of only forty-years or so, most of the industry around Trethurgy came into being. One reason for this sudden flurry of industrial activity in the middle of the 19th century was the repeal of the 'Corn Laws' in 1846. This allowed a lot of cheap foreign corn into the country and had the unfortunate effect of putting a great number of farm labourers out of work. As they were no longer required on the land, they turned to other local industries. To complete the picture, by 1909, the Clay pit at the end of Hennals lane was in production, as was Vivian's granite quarry to the west of Carn Grey. Therefore, we can state with some certainty that, with the exception of tin streaming, all of the industrial enterprises around Trethurgy came into being within 70 years and that they ceased to function by 1970.

Tin

Tin streaming was probably the earliest mining activity around Trethurgy. We have evidence of it dating back to the 2nd to 5th century AD, with discovery of the tin ingot during the excavations at Trethurgy round. The early tinners worked in open moorland and found the tin in the alluvial deposits which occurred from Pentruff, down through Trethurgy Butts; past what is now Trethurgy playing field and continuing through Hennals woods to Garker. Tin streaming consisted of using a stream of water to wash the alluvial deposits and, in doing so, removing the sand and other lighter material to reveal the tin ore. The next step was to produce sufficient charcoal to smelt the ore and then, to build a furnace to do so. As part of the Duchy Manor of Treverbyn Courtney, many tin works existed in this area. Trethurgy may well have been founded as an agricultural village, but miners cottages developed around the original farm settlement.

The earliest evidence we have on record of tin streaming around Trethurgy is found in documents stored in The Cornwall Record Office Truro.

The earliest document starts:

"To wit one Pair of Tinworks Bounds called Good Profits Bounds lying and being in Trethurgy common Cutt and Pitched the 2nd day of May 1749 by Nicholas Allen and James Watts to the only use of Philip Carlyon of Tregrehan."

A second document reads:

"Jacob Luke of St Blazey, tinner, a bill of sale of Little High Tin Bounds in Trethurgy Common the 12th April 1756 for the sum of £4—2s—0d to Philip Carlyon of Tregrehan."

The document then continues with an endearing description of the tin bounds:

"the NE corner lyeth nigh a hedge of a field called .... in possession of Philip Clarke. SE corner lyeth nigh a millpool in occupation of Nicholas Borlaze and others. The SW corner lyeth nigh or adjoining to the SW end of Butts Plosh under or nigh a hedge of a field belonging to a tenement called Alseveare. The NW corner lyeth nigh the said hedge nigh a shute or stream of water where the said Philip Clarke and his family usually take his and their pots of water."

The only piece of ground which we can identify with any certainty from the archaic description stated is that of Trethurgy common, which stretched from the 1862 Wesleyan chapel, through the present playing field and up in the direction of Carn Grey and Pentruff. The two fields to the north west of *Knightor Close* were possibly part of Alseveor Tenement, though this is by no means certain. The cottages along the lane which branches off the road at *Ruby Cottage* were known as *Butts Cottages*. The land, immediately in front of them, is referred as 'Trethurgy Butts' on the Tithe map of 1842. Interestingly, as a boy, I used to go down into the 'splosh' to fetch water from the shute which was merely an iron pipe feeding spring water into the stream and running under the road between *Rockhurst* and *Ruby Cottage*. The 'splosh' was a piece of sunken ground which lay to the rear and side of my home and was permanently wet. It is intriguing to see that these two words - i.e. 'shute' and 'splosh' - have survived almost unchanged for two hundred years.

A Mr Luke was working Pentruff for both tin and clay by the 1840s and with an annual production of some 500 tons [presumably, this refers to clay]. There is also mention of 4 tons of tin being produced in 1899. A Carn Grey tin mine was also working in the 1830s. It was sited somewhere in the area between the ruined chimney stack on the side of the road between Trethurgy and Tregonissey; and the present waste disposal and recycling site at Menear. The stack is believed to have been for the use of the mine's steam engine - probably a small beam engine.

This is as much as can be found regarding tin production. We can surmise, with reasonable accuracy, that tin streaming would have uncovered china clay and that with the clay being more abundant than the tin, this would have quite naturally superseded it. Carclaze and Pentruff mines are prime examples of this.

China Clay

Before discussing clay, we should pay tribute to William Cookworthy, who was born at Kingsbridge in Devon on 12th April, 1705. He was a man of many qualities, but is revered in Cornwall for finding clay in the St Austell area. He also discovered a way of making porcelain, which had previously been imported from China. He opened a factory for the manufacture of porcelain in Plymouth in 1768; twelve years before his death on 17th October 1780.

66

China clay, or Kaolin, was produced by washing softened granite with jets of pressurised water and resulting in a stream of sand, clay and small stones. This stream was channelled and directed so that the heavier impurities, such as sand and mica [silicates], were separated from the water. This 'white river' was then further channelled and sent on to large settling tanks which were adjacent to a kiln or clay dry.

This is the opening into the clay dry from the settling tank.
It is visible on land behind the playing field.

These tanks were eventually filled with slurry of clay by a simple process of filling them and then, allowing the clay to settle before opening a sluice to drain off the excess water. This was repeated until the tank was full of clay slurry. The slurry was then drained off and directed into a drying pan where it would be spread out evenly. When dry, it was cut into blocks and loaded onto lorries for transporting to one of the clay ports of Par or Charlestown. It should be said that this is a personal recollection from the 1940s and that all the work I had witnessed was done by hand at the clay dry at Garker. The sand and other waste from the washing process were loaded into a v-shaped skip which was then hauled up an inclined tramway by means of a stationary engine. The rear of the skip was released at the top to deposit its load and resulted in the forming of the cone shaped mounds of sand which has given rise to Cornwall being referred as the 'land of the white pyramids'.

As was previously stated, Pentruff was originally worked by a Mr Luke in the 1840s. In 1863, the Martin Brothers inherited Pentruff from their mother and produced tin and clay. In 1884, Parkyn and Peters took over Pentruff; by which time, the main workings had probably settled at the final pit site. The stack, which served the

horizontal steam engine, still stands on the south side of the pit. The small clay dry that is located just beyond the Trethurgy playing field, served Pentruff in its early years. It ceased to function when clay was piped to a new dry at Par Moor which was built in 1914. Pentruff finally closed in 1942, as part of the war-time consolidation of the China Clay Industry. The clay dry at Trethurgy has almost lost its identity and is fast becoming just a pile of ruined masonry amidst a jungle of willows, briars and marshy ground. When approached from the playing field, the two large furnaces, or ovens, are still clearly visible and a scramble around to the right of them will reveal the remains of the flues which directed the heat beneath the drying pan.

Trethurgy Stack in the 1990s

The chimney stack is still visible from the playing field. In facing the stack, on the left hand side are two settling tanks. These are both in quite a good state of preservation and with their sluice gates being clearly visible. One tank has only one opening or sluice gate; the others, have three. Also, on this side, were the supports that held one half of the roof, if memory serves me correctly. On the right hand side are a number of granite pillars which supported the other half. The chimney at the other end is only just visible

through the vegetation and almost completely covered in ivy.

The Lantern China Clay Co. was created in 1899, with the shareholders being Lewis Holder, Augustus Holder, Caroline Holder and Laura Holder, all from Whitehaven in Cumberland; also, John Fletcher from Liverpool and Rees Keene from Gosforth. This company was worth £8,000 in 1899. In 1936, the company moved to the clay pit at Hennals, but retained its name and was certainly still operating as 'The Lantern China Clay Co.' between 1945 and 1950 under the ownership of Mr. Molyneaux. He was a well respected figure in the community and used to fund the Christmas party in the old school hall. Around this time, another pit was opened, but it never reached productivity. Sometime later, concrete blocks were produced here and again, I remember watching this process. It was very simple with a mixture of sand, cement and water being turned over several times by two or three men using long-handled Cornish shovels. The result was a fairly 'dry mix' that was packed into metal moulds. These were then upended to leave the 'green' block to dry and harden. Tom Seward recalls that the first man producing concrete blocks was Kitchener Grose and he was followed by the Bray brothers. The block works finally closed in the early 1970s.

Ruby, Knightor and Treverbyn Iron Mines

These three mines - all within half a mile of each other - were situated on the Ruby iron lode. This lode or vein of iron stretches from the south coast, near to Crinnis Island and northwards to the parish of Withiel, a distance of nine miles. Where it enters Trethurgy, the ore is described as being of remarkable purity; with some picked samples containing 96.2% of iron peroxide. The Wheal Ruby shaft was situated some 350 yards north west of Trethurgy and occupied the third field down from *'Knightor Manor'* towards the village.

This, and another shaft, were still visible in the 1940s; the other, lying just above the shute or spring that is the source of the stream under the road adjacent to *Ruby Cottage*. These mine workings from the 1840s to 1894, though not continuously, were certainly profitable.

Here is a quote from Royal Cornwall Gazette of 27th January 1865.

One Moiety* of a Valuable Iron Mine for Sale.

William Hancock has received instructions to Sell by Public Auction on Tuesday the fourteenth day of February next, at three-o-clock in the afternoon, at Dunns Hotel, St Austell,

in the County of Cornwall [subject to such conditions as will be then and there produced] 256/512ths Parts of Shares of and in all that well known and extensive Iron Mine known as WHEAL RUBY AND KNIGHTOR IRON MINE, situate in the county and parish aforesaid. The shares will be sold in one or more lots, as may be agreed on at the time of the sale.. It further states that the "ore raised is about a thousand tons a month and that this will be increased, the mine is making good profits, and the cost of carriage from the mine to the ports of Par and Charlestown is averaging only one shilling and nine pence [eight new pence] per ton.
[* Moiety = a half]

There is also a clipping from the Daily Telegraph of 1872; referring to the iron mine at Knightor which dealt with the selling of shares and, as a further inducement, stated that there were plans to build a tram line to St Austell station. However, there is no evidence of this line ever being constructed. When searching for the output of these mines, there is a reference to Wheal Ruby and, slightly puzzling, the inclusion of a mine called 'Trethurgy'. Careful checking of the 1882 Ordnance survey shows Treverbyn, Knightor and Wheal Ruby mines, but no mention of a Trethurgy mine!

About half way through the mines' history, the owner, Mr Allott, became bankrupt. Below, are some newspaper cuttings at that time:

THE BANKRUPTCY OF MR. ALFRED ALLOTT.— This gentlemen, a large coal and iron proprietor at Sheffield, who failed a few weeks ago for £210,000, was, it appears, also the owner of the Ruby and Trethurgy Iron mines in Cornwall, carried on as the " Ruby and Trethurgy Iron mines Company." The debts contracted in connection with the Cornwall Company amount to £9,194, distributed among 45 creditors. The largest item in the list, £8,000, is due to the Credit Foncier of England. The remainder is due mostly to Cornish people for supplies to the mine. To Mr. E. Faulconer, St. Austell, £396 ; Ivimey and Gill, London, £450 ; William and Anne Nicholls, St. Austell, £150 ; H. J. Andrew, St. Austell, £17 ; Frederick Jenkin, Biscovey, £11 ; Richard Martyn, St. Austell, £75. The remaining items are all under £5.

THE AFFAIRS OF ALDERMAN ALLOTT.
LIABILITIES, £210,000.

We regret to announce that yesterday afternoon a petition for the liquidation of his affairs was filed by Ald. Alfred Allett, of Brincliffe Grove and Norfolk street, Sheffield, accountant. The liabilities are estimated at about £210,000, of which some £170,000 are fully secured. Mr. Jarvis W. Barber (of the firm of Barber Bros. and Wortley) has been appointed receiver. Mr. Allott has been for some time struggling to sustain engagements entered into during the prosperous times of 1872 and 1873. The depression that has followed has, however, been so severe and protracted that he has now found it necessary to take the extreme step named.

In his petition Mr. Allott sets forth that he is a public accountant, lately carrying on business at Sheffield in co-partnership with Thomas Hadfield and John Kidner, under the firm of Alfred Allott and Company; also carrying on business as a colliery proprietor in Brightside, formerly in partnership with John Crossley, under the firm of the Pitsmoor Coal Company, and now carrying on the business of an ironmaster at the Renishaw Ironworks, at Eckington, in partnership with James Morrison, William Hunter, Hilton Philipson, Henry Tennant, and the executors of William John Hutchinson, deceased, under the firm of Appleby and Co., also carrying on business in the county of Northampton, under the firm of the New Bridge Iron Ore Company, and at St. Austell, in Cornwall, as an iron mine proprietor, under the firm of the Ruby and Trethurgy Mine Company.

3rd.—Separate Creditors of the said ALFRED ALLOTT, in respect of the business carried on by him under the style of "THE RUBY AND TRETHURGY IRON MINE COMPANY."

	£	s.	d.
Andrew, H. J., rate collector, St. Austell, Cornwall	17	19	1½
Andrew, James, stationer, St. Austell, Cornwall	0	3	3
Bennett, J., bootmaker, Luxulyan, Cornwall	3	18	0
Borlace, John, Carwallen, nr. St. Austell, Cornwall	0	19	6
Beard, J., Trethurgy, near St. Austell, Cornwall	5	10	0
Coode, Shilson & Co., solicitors, St. Austell Cornwl	0	3	5½
Carlyon & Stephens, solicitors, St. Austell, Cornwl	0	1	7
Clark, John, Carn Gray, St. Austell, Cornwall	3	13	4
Credit Foncier of England, Limited, London	8000	0	0
Devon and Cornwall Bank, St. Austell, Cornwall	15	0	0
Faulconer, Edward, St. Austell, Cornwall	395	0	0
Giles Philip, stationer, St. Austell, Cornwall	1	10	0
Hawke, G., and Co., hardwaremen, St. Austell	0	3	6
Hocking, Thomas, Bethel, near St. Austell	2	1	0
Hancock, Joseph, Union rd., St. Austell	1	11	0
Hore, Elizabeth, Higher Gray Farm, Trethurgy	3	7	0
Hembly, John, sawyer, Tywardreath Par Station	1	3	6
Ivimey and Gill, 18, Bedford place, London	450	0	0
Jenkin, Frederick, Biscovay, St. Austell	11	13	0
Julyan, Joseph, Roscorla, St. Austell, Cornwall	2	6	0
Kingdon, James, Sen., Trethurgy, near St. Austell	0	15	6
Knight, P., and Son, merchants, St. Austell	1	18	5
Kingdon, James, Jun., Trethurgy, near St. Austell	2	8	0
Luke, Jane, Trethurgy, near St. Austell, Cornwall	0	7	1
Martyn, Richard, St. Austell, Cornwall	75	0	0
Moss, S., and Co., Merchants, Par, Cornwall	3	5	10
Mumiar, John, Tregonissey, St. Austell, Cornwall	2	5	9
Mugford, Michael, Trethurgy, nr St. Austell, Corn	3	11	6
Marshall, W. Henry, mason, Mount Charles, Corn	0	5	6
Nicholls, Wm., St. Austell, Cornwall	} 150	0	0
Nicholls, Ann, Trustees of, Hancock and others			
Nankwell, Joseph, Grampound road, Cornwall	2	13	4
Pearce, Walter, Brittannia, Cornwall	2	11	9
Parnell, John, Charlestown, St. Austell, Cornwall	2	2	3
Parks, John, Roselyon, St. Blazey Gate, Cornwall	0	5	6
Rowett, Richd., Phoenissick, Tregonissey, Cornwall	1	3	0

These tonnages are taken from a paper written by a Mr Collings and dated 1912. It states:-

Trethurgy   Wheal Ruby

1847   sold 136 tons of copper ore from intersection of a copper lode.

1862   sold 2,000 tons of iron ore.

1864-71   sold 44,700 tons of iron ore. (Partly from Knightor mine)

1872-80   sold 25,150 tons. (Partly from Trethurgy mine)

What springs to mind when reading these figures is that Trethurgy must have been a bustling little place in the mid to late 1800s, having produced 72,000 tons of iron ore in approximately 18 years. Also, let us not forget that this iron ore had to be transported to the coast by horse and cart. This would imply that there must have been some stabling and blacksmithing facilities nearby; not to mention, stores of water and fodder. Sadly, all of this came to an end in the winter of 1892-93 when a claim for 'unpaid wages' was lodged with the Stannery court.

17th November 1892.

In the court of the Vice Warden of the Stannaries is a claim by various miners against William Nicholls of St Austell - Local Purser, Head Manager and agent of the Knightor and Ruby Iron Mine for unpaid wages. The claimants were Isaac Coon of Chytan Trethurgy and others.

ACCOUNT OF WAGES UNPAID reads as follows:-

		£	s	d
Isaac Coon		2	10	0
------------- 3 wks to June 25th		3	15	0
------------- 9 wks half pay up to August 27th 1892		5	12	6
Abraham I Warne	3 days	0	10	0
Joseph Trethewey	2 days		6	8
William Trethewey	3 days		10	0
Thomas Hancock	3 days		10	0
Jonathon Blandford	4 days		12	0
Harry White	2 days		6	0
John Morstead	6 days	1	00	0
Richard Medlin	6 days		4	0
Horse and Cart	3 days at 4/-		12	0
Field Gate			6	0
J H Rowe	3 days at 4/-		12	0
Nicholas Colling	3 days at 1/-		3	0
John Creba	for steelwork	1	14	1
Total		£19	3s	2d

William Nicholls was summoned by the court to appear within 8 days to show why he should not be ordered to pay for work done by the claimants at Knightor and Ruby iron mine. The summons was served on Mr Nicholls by Robert Dobell, a solicitor, of 9 Pydar Street, Truro, on the 18th November 1892. There followed an examination of the necessary documents to the effect that Mr Nicholls had to pay all the claimants' court costs, plus the unpaid wages.

To further complicate matters, there then appeared a document dated 26th November 1892 from the landlords, Ivemey & Gill, stating that they were owed £90 for unpaid rent by a John Hallway of Jeffreys Square, London, who had occupied the mine and premises; and that the bailiff of the Stannary Court was not to remove any of the mine materials until that rent was paid. To cut a long story short, the Stannery Court restrained the landlords from selling any of the mines' machinery. It was, however, later sold on behalf of the miners on 1st February 1893. Some of the machinery actually belonged to a Mr R D Warne, who received £1/18/1. The remainder raised was £6/1/0.

The final document stated that the court demand in the name of 'Her Majesty the Queen' that the defendant pay the claim plus all costs. What the final outcome was we do not know, but it is obvious that considerable hardship was felt by these men; since, not only had they lost their jobs at the mine, but were waiting from August 1892 to the following February for their wages.

Looking back on these events, we can see there was a great need for some formal regulation from the government and that the ordinary working man would have to unite to defend himself from such exploitation.

The Stannary Court

The stanneries were the tin mining districts of Cornwall and Devon and, from antiquity, had produced a very independent class of worker. In 1201, King John issued a charter which granted tinners' rights to mark boundaries in their name and to stream for tin; with a warden appointed to oversee jurisdiction and to collect revenues. Over the years, and granting of several royal charters and various acts of parliament, the stannaries had become a state within a state. They had their own courts, their own laws and their own parliament. They acknowledged no lord and obeyed only the king when his orders were transmitted through their warden. Initially, they had jurisdiction only over tinners but, with the passage of time, their control increased to include all mining activities. In 1896, the stannary courts were abolished and their powers transferred to the Cornwall County Court.

Granite Quarries

Carn Grey, near St Austell, became one of the four main Hensbarrow granite quarries. The granite had a fine even grain and was in much demand for the construction of imposing public buildings, such as 'The Market House' in St Austell and other similar buildings further afield.

The Treffry estate had the quarry from 1847 and was paying the rent ten years later to prevent it from being worked by any rival. There were fears that the Tor [Carn Grey Rock] would be destroyed by quarrying in 1869, but these fears were said to be unfounded by the then quarrier, Thomas Gill.

Later on, in the 1880s, the quarry was owned by the Freemans and, according to the 1882 ordnance survey map, there were now two quarries. They were known as the 'top quarry' - the one lying immediately below Carn Grey Rock - and the 'bottom quarry' - situated lower down and much closer to the roadside. There was a third quarry in the moor, west of Carn Grey, which probably commenced operating in the late 1880s. This was owned and operated by the Vivian brothers - Joseph, Henry, Harry, Jacob and Alfred - who were granite merchants. Known variously as West Carn Grey, Pentruff Quarry and Vivians Quarry, it produced the stone for the St Austell Public Rooms in Truro Road. On one side of the quarry, the stone was slightly pink and quite distinctive. In January of 1922, the Vivians, who had previously used black powder for blasting the rock, started using high explosives. This was to the detriment of the neighbours, Parkyn and Peters, who worked the nearby Pentruff clay pit. The Vivians were the defendants in a dispute from which this quote is taken:

"From this time Parkyn and Peters have from time to time complained that stones were thrown into their China Clay Works to the danger of themselves, their employees and their workmen. Also, by reason of such splinters and stones,

the clay produced by them lying in their tanks has been damaged or deteriorated and the buildings of the Plaintiffs (Parkyn and Peters) damaged by such splinters."

A writ was issued, in July 1922, with Parkyn and Peters claiming damages for loss and asking for an injunction to restrain the Vivian Brothers from:

Quote: "..... so working the said quarry as to endanger the employees or property of the Plaintiffs in or about their said China Clay Works."

The outcome of this dispute was an agreement between the two parties which stated that the Vivians would pay the costs of the action, which was £35, and that in future, they would not use high explosives in their quarry. This document was signed by Joseph Henry Vivian and Harry Vivian on 22nd May, 1923. Subsequently, the Vivians sold their quarry to Claude Selleck in 1924; though they continued working there up to the 1930s. The accompanying map, dated 8th April 1914, formed part of an agreement between Ivemey & Gill, the landlords, and Parkyn & Peters, to work in Pentruff for clay and tin. This map shows the close proximity of the Vivians' quarry to the Pentruff clay works. This quarry was buried beneath the tip to the east of Carclaze pit during the 1970s.

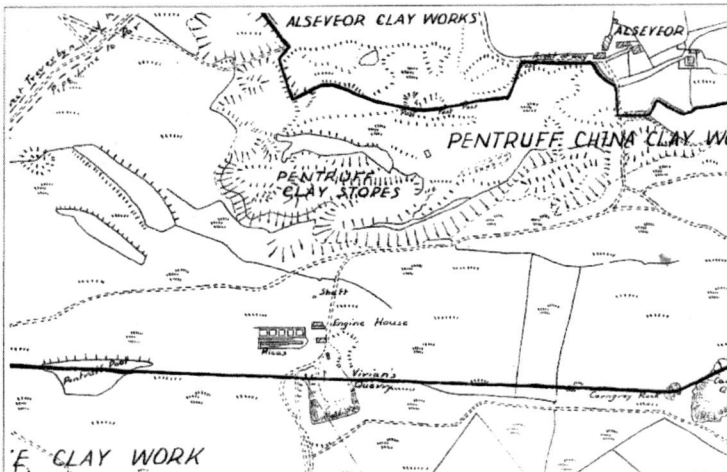

Returning to the two Carn Grey quarries; tramways, of 18in gauge, connected them and this, is clearly visible on the 1882 OS map. There are still traces of them to be found between the two quarries, as seen in the photograph below.

The bottom quarry supplied a lot of stone for Devonport Docks around 1900. Later on, in the mid-1920s, it was supplying crushed stone for tarmac and ballast on the new St Austell by-pass.

The tar plant was located just below the bottom quarry and on the same side of the road. There was a jaw crusher; three trammel screens and a tar macadam plant, which were driven by a steam engine with a portable horizontal boiler. It is claimed that Claude Selleck was running out of good stone reserves and intended to quarry Carn Grey rock and the stone beneath it. However, there was such an outcry against this proposed vandalism that the scheme was abandoned.

Up until about 1933/34, the blast hole drilling was done by hand. Claude Selleck, who owned the quarries, had a building erected to house an air compressor which would drive a compressed air jack hammer. Blasting in the bottom quarry ceased very early in the 1930s, due largely to local complaints of flying rock.

Almost all of this information has come via John Tonkin of St Austell, who has a particular interest in local history and especially, that of mining. He further interviewed Ralph Vivian, who was a son of one of the Vivians, as previously mentioned, and had worked in the local clay and granite industries. Ralph stated that during the 1920s, he worked for Claude Selleck in the top quarry and in doing so, produced stone for hedging and much of the County Council kerbing. Their stone was also supplied for the building of the Dawlish stretch of railway line.

In 1931, Selleck Nicholls and Company employed 114 men at four quarries - the two Carn Grey quarries, West Carn Grey and Denders quarry at Luxulyan. The stone crusher and steam engine were relocated to the top quarry and remained there until it was removed for scrap. The foundation plinths for the stone crusher are still to be seen near the entrance to the top quarry.

In September 1936, the quarrying of stone ceased and production of various concrete products was started up and continued until the outbreak of the Second World War. During the mid-1930s, Claude Selleck moved the machinery to Denders quarry at Luxulyan. Approximately twenty years later, Henry Orchard removed the remaining 'gear' for scrap.

Many of the 'menhirs' or standing stones in the district are of Carn Grey granite and must have come from the moors near to the rock. Trethurgy owned three of these menhirs - one was in the centre of the village, in the grounds of *Moorview*. During the 1890s, this stone was used as a pedestal to hold 'disused' tins that became targets at which the village boys would throw stones. I was told this by John Julian, who lived all his life in Trethurgy. The standing stone was probably removed when the house was built in the 1920s. The second was located at the bottom of the field that lies to the left of *Chapel Lane* and which, was still standing in the 1950s. And the third was in the grounds of the cottage *Little Grey* which is on the bend of the road approaching the bottom quarry.

Personal Memories

Farming Days in 1940s by Shirley Wooders (nee Kingdon)

I remember when I helped with my father's milk round and we delivered milk to the people of Trethurgy with his horse and trap. We had two churns on the back which had taps. Hooked to the taps were quart, pint and half pint measures that we used when selling the milk. People would come out of their homes with an assortment of containers for their milk, like jugs and saucepans. One lady down in Tregrehan would bring out her teapot to be filled with milk - as a child, this seemed to be quite funny!

Our milk round took us down through Garker to Tregrehan and from there, we went up Tregrehan Hill. We also delivered to Miss Carlyon at Tregrehan House and the other houses on the Tregrehan estate. I remember seeing the prisoners of war in their camp; there were Germans and Italians. The round would continue through Liskey, Bodelva and Starrack Moor.

Sheldon and his horse were often seen around the village.

Later on, the milk was sold in glass bottles which had cardboard stoppers. I remember that we had to rinse and sterilise the bottles before placing them upside down to drain. The milk round was very much a seven days a week job!

Farm life was busy all year around. When the fields were ready to be planted, I can remember that before this was done, the hedges had to be pared and made tidy. The fields were then ploughed in readiness for the crops, such as potatoes, swedes and turnips.

The harvest was a very busy time. The local gypsies who used to work and live on the land helped throughout the year. Hay harvest was always busy, from the time it was cut to the time it was carried. Something I can vividly remember is the 'hole' that was left in the centre of the hay rick for air to circulate. I remember we always ate roast beef at harvest time and this would be washed down with tea - definitely, no alcohol! There was also another round which provided the village of Trethurgy with their daily milk - Ivy Crowle used to carry it in two buckets supported by a yoke. Later, the milk was bottled and sold to the villagers.

Trethurgy in 1945 by W B Shipley

Let me recall Trethurgy as I remember it when I arrived in August 1945 by taking you on a 'walk' around the village. My objective, in doing so, is to describe the dwellings and people at that time. Below, is a rough map on which I have numbered each property for ease of identification.

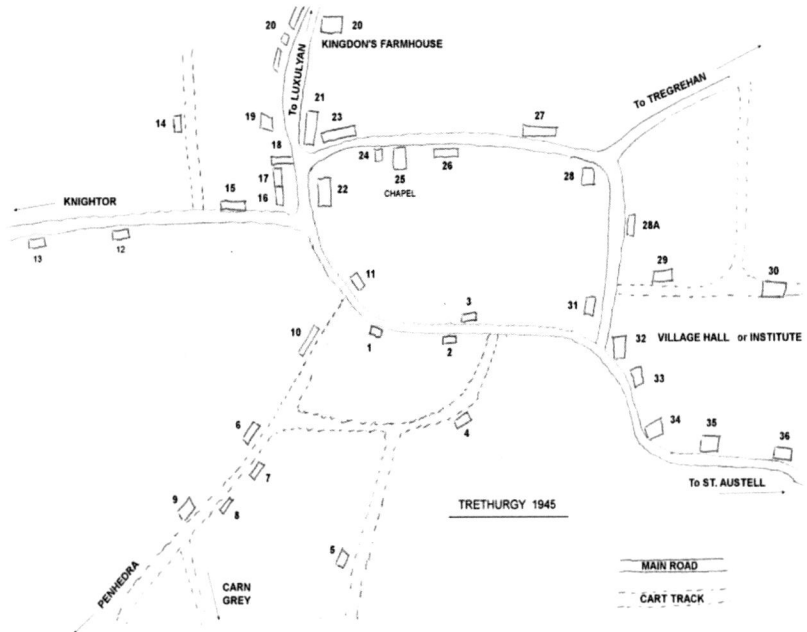

TRETHURGY 1945

Number [1] is *Ruby Cottage*, where I lived with my mother, Medea; step-father, Nelson; step-sister, Betty, and my step-gran, Charlotte. Nelson was a joiner and Betty, a shop assistant. It originally comprised of two buildings joined together in an L-shape. They were associated with the Wheal Ruby iron mine and had been used as a 'counting house' and 'drying shed' for the miners' clothing.

A later addition was added by Mrs Sandercombe in the 1880s. The mains electricity supply was installed in February 1937.

Ruby Cottage in 2012.

Walking away from *Ruby Cottage* in the direction of St. Austell, the first port of call is the *village shop* [2] which was run by Mildred Wellington. This was a wooden building and divided in two. The front half was the shop and a step down led to the rear which acted both as a rest room and store. It contained a small table, a couple of chairs, plus a primus stove and all the necessary items for making a cup of tea. The local folk would meet there for a chat and 'cuppa' with the water for the tea being supplied from a spring or 'chute' that was close by. Mildred lived in *Restineas Cottage* down at Garker and had two sisters, Audrey and Gladys, who both lived nearby.

Next [3] - opposite to the shop, is the house where Mrs Trevail and her son, Jack, lived. She was an elderly lady and he did not work. They were eventually forcibly evicted by bailiffs. They and their belongings ended up on a patch of vacant ground to the south of the house. In 1947/48, the house was occupied by a retired police superintendent named Truscott; his wife and daughter, Pauline, who was a registered nurse. They had one of only two cars in the village at that time – the other, belonged to Hayden Luke of Knightor Manor.

In walking past this house and turning right up a lane, we come to [4] where Margie Webber and her husband, Dick, lived with their son, Horace. This house and its land were divided by the lane. On the opposite side to the house was their large garden which they used for growing vegetables and fruit and also, having a chicken run, plus a garage. The garden was divided from *Ruby Cottage* by a small valley, approximately 10-12 ft deep and some 20 ft across. There were a number of these 'cuttings' in the area, which appeared to be linked with several old mine shafts.

Turning left into another lane leads to [5]. Here lived Bill Bennett, his wife, Ida, and their 6 children - Alan, Marjorie, Roger, Sylvia, Michael, and Aubrey. They had a very long strip of ground which was most productive. As well as being self-sufficient in vegetables; Bill also kept pigs and hens. Theirs was probably the largest garden in the village.

Immediately in front of their home was a small river that ran down past the Webbers, under the road and across a piece of waste ground towards the Chapel. It continued under another road and down towards Hennals wood and the Lantern china clay works, where Marjorie Bennett worked as a secretary. In front of their house just on the other side of the river was a sand barrow and beyond this, a disused clay dry with 3 or 4 settling tanks. Back-tracking down 'Bennett's lane', we then turn left for a short distance before following a fork to the left.

This brings us to a cottage [6] on the right, which was occupied by the Dewings family who were staunch 'Methodists'. The flower arranging at the chapel was shared between them and others. A story goes that there was an altercation over some flower arranging and due to this, the Dewings left Trethurgy chapel and formed their own group of worship that was joined by others who lived outside of Trethurgy. They would actually meet in their own houses for worship. From memory, I believe that the women folk wore black or dark blue stockings.

Next up the lane, on the left, was a pair of semi-detached houses [7]. The first called *Gloucester House* belonged to Bert Mugford and his wife, Doris; and next door, lived Ray Hamley, a widower. The surface of the lane was now composed of large smooth blocks of granite instead of sand and gravel. This more permanent surface ceases as we come to *Alseveor Cottage* [8] which was a small-holding occupied by Bill and Violet Ridge, their daughter, Vanda, and Violet's mother, Annie Julian, whose husband, Pheppy, had been captain of the Bodelva Clay Pit [now, of 'Eden Project' fame] and Pentruff Clay Pit. Next, on the right and a few yards along, we come to [9] which is *Alseveor Farm* and worked by Sammy Tonkin and his wife. Two of their fields were above land owned by the Bennetts' family and, as a consequence, Michael, Aubrey and I were constantly trespassing and being chased away by Sammy.

My memory of him is that he wore an apron and a shawl of sack-cloth that was fastened by a length of twine. According to Shirley Kingdon, this was common practise among people who worked on the land. The apron was of a lighter sacking than the shawl, as it merely kept the trousers clean; whereas, the shawl was of a much heavier material and slightly greasy, so as to keep the rain at bay.

The lane then divides again, left towards Carn Grey Rock and the quarries and, to the right, across the moor towards *Penhedra Farm* where the Nancarrow family lived. Their children were Pamela, Marylou, Mervyn, John and Richard. Coming back down the lane again, we reach the first fork mentioned at [6]. Going straight on, we arrive at [10]. This building, known as *Butts Cottage,* comprised of three dwellings - the first was occupied by a single man who was a baker; then the next, by George Rundle, his wife, Miriam, and their two boys, Keith and Peter; and finally, Warren and Gladys Wedlake, who were, later, joined by Geoffrey Liddicoate.

Next to this cottage was a large corrugated iron shed which served as a workshop and 'makeshift' barbers. Warren was foreman of a road maintenance gang, but he also acted as the village barber. A boy's haircut cost sixpence in those days, but the hand clippers would occasionally pull out a tuft of hair which made it quite an enlivening experience! At one stage, Warren decided to keep a pig, but it wormed its way into his affections to such an extent that, when it was sent for slaughter, it broke his heart and he never kept another. George Rundle was a lorry driver, as was Bill Bennett.

If we carry on down the lane where it joins the road; just to the left was the milk churn collection point, which consisted of a platform constructed of railway sleepers. Bill Ridge and Sammy Tonkin had to deliver their milk churns to this collection point all the way from *Alseveor Farm* which was about half a mile away. On the opposite side of the road is [11] - *Rose Cottage* and home to old Mrs Gregory and possibly, her son, Bill, who was a bachelor. Shortly after I arrived, the couple moved to *Rock Cottage* to live with Jim Gregory and his son, Rodney. Walking towards the village, there is a large field on the left that is bounded, on the roadside, by a stone wall and topped with iron railings [now, *Knightor Close*]. There was a post box built into the wall just as the road curves left towards *Knightor Manor*. Taking this road for about 50 yards, we come to a small complex [12] - comprising of a house that was converted into two flats and a cottage. The lower flat was occupied by Jack and Winnie Chapman and their son, Brian. In the upper flat, lived Wilf and May Keam, with daughter, Marjorie, and later, in 1951, Kathryn. To the rear, in *Rock Cottage* lived Jim Gregory and his son, Rodney, together with his mother and brother, Bill.

Walking along this road for a quarter of a mile or so, we come to *Knightor Manor* [13] where Hayden Luke and his wife lived. He was our 'unofficial' squire and owned the first car in the village. Mr Luke was held in great esteem by all and sundry. Behind Knightor, is a lane leading to the cottage of Ed and Florrie Williams, who had two daughters, Maureen and Theresa. Ed worked on Knightor farm and was the son of Ephraim.

This is our boundary, so we now turn around and head back to the crossroads. After passing the last field on the left, which is the site of the original Methodist chapel, we arrive at a couple of barns and then, turn up a lane leading to a cottage [14] where George and Winnie Ronaldson and their 5 children - Lewis, Betty, Dennis, Sylvia and Preston lived. Lewis later became a mechanic; Betty was a shop assistant and, I believe, George worked in the clay industry.

Going back down this lane and turning left onto the road, we arrive at two cottages [15] with small front gardens. The first was occupied by Jean and George Orchard and their children. The second belonged to John and Fred Allen and their sister, Emma Jane. Poor John fell on some ice by the village tap and broke his hip. He was taken to St. Austell hospital, where, sadly, he died about a week later. I recall that Fred once chased a group of us boys a mile or more across fields and hedges down to Starrick moor. This was caused by us playing football outside his cottage.

We turn left again, at the crossroads, and head towards *Trethurgy Farm*. On the left is [16], representing two cottages. The first was inhabited by George Elwood, a chief petty officer in the navy; his wife, May, and daughter, Marjory. This building is said to be the oldest in the village and, according to local lore, was once an 'ale-house'. The second of these two cottages housed a Mr and Mrs Fitzpatrick. Next, in house [17] lived Mr and Mrs Julian. He lived all his life in Trethurgy and his wife was Welsh. They had a remarkable table - it seemed to me, at 8 years old, to contain everything - clothes, books, food, groceries, cakes, pans and other assorted items. They had a daughter called Joan Payne, who had married and moved away. Mr Julian once told me that the wooden chapel, which had preceded the present one, had been situated close to the road in the first field on the right hand side heading up towards *Knightor Manor*. However, no trace of this remains. The Julian's garden was bounded on the right by a couple of ruined cottages [18] located at right angles to the road and with the gable on the road side. Carrying straight on, to the left is *The Elms* [19] - a house set back from the road and where Ellen Kingdon [Sheldon's mother] lived. We have now reached [20], with the Kingdon's farm buildings on the left and their farmhouse and yard on the right. Sheldon and Ernestine farmed here. They had three children, Shirley, Rhona and Jeffrey. Sheldon's mother, Ellen, was a sister of Dick and Pheppy Julian.

We turn back here, as we have reached our limit in this direction. So, in leaving the farm on the left, the next two cottages [21] comprise of two 'one-up one-down' dwellings where Mr and Mrs Garland lived and, alongside them, Mrs Tregidga and her son, George. It was Mrs

Garland who took the trouble to initiate me into the correct way to make tea. I should add that I was a frequent visitor, as my Grandmother and various others, including Mrs Garland swapped 'True Love Stories' and of which, the less said, the better! These two cottages were approached by a narrow path from *Chapel Lane,* which led between them and the gable end of a further ruin – this being [23]. They were destroyed by fire in the 1950s and, apart from the gable end of the ruin which is still standing, nothing else remains of these buildings.

On the opposite side of Chapel Lane is *Moorland House* [22] that belonged to a retired Major Webb, who lived with his wife and daughter, Auriole. His wife suffered with extreme ill health and could be heard screaming for long periods, especially at night. She was conveyed in a wheelchair. Mr Webb owned three small fields, opposite to *Ruby Cottage*, where he kept several goats. Every so often, these animals needed their hooves trimming. The drill was that two or three boys would round up the goats and 'Webby', as we called him, would entice them into the milking shed with the aid of a carrot. He then trimmed their hooves as a couple of boys held on to the goat. These animals were kept for their milk and meat. Sheldon Kingdon was paid one shilling to kill; skin and butcher them and afterwards, they would be stored in a deep freeze cabinet. Mr Webb was a very polite, mild-mannered and well-spoken man, who had all our sympathies.

We next turn down the road leading towards the chapel. On the left hand side, immediately after *Tregidgas Cottage,* are two or three ruined cottages [23] on the roadside pointing downhill. On the left, at the bottom of the hill, is the lane leading to Ennals wood and the Lantern china clay works. A family of gypsies lived down there – the father was called Bill Crocker. They had four sons: Tom, Jimmy, Billy and Norman and would move camp from time to time. Opposite to this lane is *The Sunday School* [24] which also served as a venue for concerts, feasts and the annual Christmas party which was funded by Mr Molyneaux, the owner of the Lantern china clay works. Alongside the Sunday school is the *Wesleyan Chapel* [25] which was built in 1862. This was the centre of village life and the venue at which most of the decisions regarding any social events were made. Next to the chapel, on the right hand side of the road, is [26] owned by Mr and Mrs Rescorla and their children, Bernard, Joy, David and Desmond. My only memory of this place is of watching a pig being killed. Arthur Trevains had a licence and we all watched as the animal, protesting loudly, was dragged from its sty; hauled on to a table; held firmly and then killed, with its life-force gushing into a bucket. The blood was later used to make 'black pudding'. When the pig finally stopped struggling; boiling water was poured over it and the bristles removed. An incision was then made down its belly and it was hauled up by its back legs; whereupon, its inners descended onto the table. I can still remember that warm sweet smell! The cleaning and dissecting went on for a long time and I remember walking home in the dark, feeling sorry for Mr Pig!

Returning to our journey, we walk up a gentle slope and, after passing an out-building and three pony traps, we come to a cottage [27] that belonged to Ephraim Williams. He was known to all as 'Eiffy'. He had a pony and cow and also, kept animals in a field next to *Bay View*.

Eiffy married for a second time, late in life; his wife being an elderly lady who only had one eye. For us children, the empty sunken lid, where her other eye should have been, held a horrid fascination! When his marriage took place, the preacher had great difficulty in persuading Eiffy to say *"I do!"* instead of *"yes sir!"*

In passing Eiffy's cottage, we then come to [28] - *Chytan Farm*. This

was owned by Sylvainus and Gertrude Ford. They lived there with daughter, Marion, and were assisted by Uncle Charlie, who lived in a caravan in the field next to Eiffy's cottage. Uncle Charlie had served with the 'Cornish Pioneers' in the First World War and was wounded in service on 1st December 1917, just before he was due on leave.

There is a fork in the road here; with the left turning leading down to Garker. Taking the right fork, we arrive at a piece of waste ground on the left that is much lower than the road. In this 'hollow' was an old fashioned style caravan [28a] where Phoebe Bull lived on her own; she could neither read nor write. There was a cart track from the road which passed across this ground and lead to [29] - a cottage where Les and Elsie Roberts lived. They had nine children: Doreen, Barbara, May, Norman, Clarence, Richard, Christine, Margaret, and Reginald. Elsie Roberts and Phyllis Hicks were sisters. That cottage is now known as *Little Grey Cottage*.

Walking down this track, we arrive at Hambly's *Hills Farm* [30]. Lottie and her husband and son, Harold, who delivered our milk, lived here, together with Freda Hancock and her son, David. Returning to the road and turning left, we reach [31] - *Bay View* which was owned by the Julians - Dick, and his wife, Ellen, and home to their daughter, Ivy Crowle, her husband, Arthur, and their daughter, Margaret. Dick was Pheppy Julian's brother and their sister, Ellen Kingdon, lived up at *The Elms*. Dick built *Bay View* but also, rented nine/ten acres of ground on the other side of the village. My abiding memory of him is walking past *Ruby Cottage* carrying two buckets of milk, which descended from a shoulder yoke via two chains.

Some fifty yards further on, we arrive at a small triangular piece of grass where three roads meet. Here, is a signpost pointing back down the road towards Tregrehan; to the right to Luxulyan and straight on to St Austell, in which direction we are now going. This brings us to [32] the *Village Institute* that was used for various social functions. The Saturday night dance was its chief source of income in the 1940s when it was also used as a primary school for two or three years. The teacher was Miss Mitchell. Michael Bennett remembers a rumbling noise coming from the boiler that would interrupt the lessons from time to time. There were two Christmas parties held in Trethurgy - one at the Sunday school and one here, in the Institute. I recall them both as tremendously exciting events.

Leaving the institute we come to [33] - a cottage belonging to John and Mary Job, who had two children - Jonnie and Jinny, although I believe her correct name was Victoria. Mr Job was a porter at Luxulyan. At the rear of this cottage, is a smaller cottage with one-up and one-down. In the bedroom, lived Louie Floyd and her daughter, Edith. They both appeared to be bedridden, although Edith did some exercise by walking around outside at night. I should add that these two ladies were also on my delivery list of 'True Love Stories'.

Next up the road, on the left, is [34]. This cottage is on the road side as it bends up the hill - Arthur and Hilda Trevains and their son, Billy, lived here. Arthur was the proud owner of a motor bike and sidecar. And, further on up the hill, on the right hand side, is the lower of two granite quarries. As we continue up the hill, we arrive at two semi-detached houses [35]. The first was occupied by Nellie Bartlett and her husband, Ned, who was confined to a wheel-chair. They had three sons - Gordon, Stan and Fred. The second property housed Bill Hicks and his wife and daughter, Valerie. Carrying on a little way further, to the right is a cart track that leads to another quarry. On the edge of this is a huge granite outcrop called *Carn Grey* - a much noted landmark which I believe was used by mariners.

A stone crusher and engine house were both situated between the two quarries. This quarry and the crusher were still working in the early 1940s but, by 1945, all work here had ceased. Lastly, along this road and to the left is [36] - a farm belonging to the Uren family who had three children - Hilda, Katy and Bill. This is as far as we go and our tour around Trethurgy comes to an end.

However, I have forgotten to mention the Crockers - Bill and his wife and their sons, Tom, Jimmy and Norman. They lived in various locations; although I only remember them living at the bottom of a field about half way down the lane towards Hennals wood. They mended things and made clothes pegs out of hazel twigs and strips of corned beef tins.

Before I sign off, I must mention the hedging and ditching man who we usually met riding his bicycle as we walked home from school. He was a tall, thin, fit man and his greeting was a raised hand followed by the exclamation "What you!" This was not being said as a query, but just his way of saying "Hallo!" He always carried a shovel and hoe strapped to his bicycle, together with a paring hook, sharpening stone and hazel stick poking out of the satchel on his back. What he was called, or where he lived, I have no idea! Valerie Hicks and Marjorie Keam, both recall another hedging and ditching man, called Howard Coade, who came from Penwithick and had swollen knobbly fingers. Margaret Crowle and Shirley Kingdon told me that he eventually moved into a cottage that was vacated by the Roberts' family.

My life in Trethurgy by Shelia Thorn (nee Orchard)

I lived in Trethurgy with my mother and three sisters. The fourth was born when we moved. We lived in the cottage near to the telephone box. The Western National bus often turned and waited outside our front garden as it didn't always go as far as Luxulyan.

I would visit my aunt Margery, who lived at Carn Cross, once a week. I used to ride with our butcher, Mr Dowe, in his van, often standing between the seats as he drove. I must have been about four years old at the time. My aunt would walk me back to the bottom of the hill in the evening and stand and watch whilst waving until I was out of sight.

One of my memories is of Feast Day when we dressed in fancy frocks and led by Bugle band, starting from the Sunday school, danced the floral dance round the village and up to Knightor Manor where we had tea followed by races and games. Aunt Gert from Chytan Farm dolloped out the cream on to huge bread splits with lashings of homemade jam on them. We, of course, had a huge saffron bun which we usually took home as it was too big to eat in one go! There were usually two sittings for tea and the gipsy boys would sit down with the first lot and still be there when the second sitting was finishing.

I also recall the 'Coronation Day' very clearly, as we had a special presentation of a mug from the Sunday school and I still have it today. One year, Effey Williams' wife, who was blind in one eye, gave both my sister and me a huge rag doll each. It was something to do with being made for or by the blind. The dolls were very beautifully made and dressed very well, in fact, very professionally. She also gave my eldest sister, Rosalind, the story of 'Cinderella'.

We lived next door to Fred and Henrietta Allen. She was a school teacher at Carclaze School. I remember that they had a mahogany table which had newspapers tied around the legs, so that we children didn't kick it when we sat in the window seat swinging our legs. All their food was hung in baskets from the ceiling to prevent the mice from getting to it. We were often given stale Christmas cake which we kept 'for later' and fed it to the horse up the road. The couple fell out quite a lot and went for ages without talking to each other. When Fred had finished a cup of tea, he would turn the cup upside down in the saucer, as a sign that he didn't want any more. They came from a wealthy family. When in his eighties and living on his own, Fred was robbed of four hundred pounds from which he never really recovered.

I can remember the sounds of Trethurgy. One of them was Sheldon Kingdon shouting at the cows (and everyone else!) when taking them in for milking; usually about 10-o-clock at night, out in the road and with a hurricane lamp. I also remember Mr Webb who was a real gentleman and always wore a trilby hat. He would take each household a quarter of tea at Christmas. Mr Webb also kept goats for milking which he kept himself, although sometimes, the boys in the village got there first. He had an eccentric daughter who wore a crinoline dress with a purse on strings. She wore her long hair up and it was filled with combs. She was always out walking with her dachshunds.

On the corner of the road by Chapel lane were two semi-detached cottages. The one nearest to our house was owned by Polly Tregidga. She was elderly and bed-ridden. It was my job, a couple of times a day, to take water to her. I would fetch it in a bucket from the tap on the wall outside of our house. I was not very old and could only carry a small amount, but it must have been enough for her needs. My father did a lot of things for her and was repeatedly offered paintings and other beautiful things. But he always refused, as he felt he was only being neighbourly. Not long after, there was a fire and she died in her cottage with all the lovely things she owned.

Memories of Margaret Hocking (nee Crowle)

I was born at 'Bay View' in Trethurgy in 1936 and lived with my mum and dad, Ivy and Arthur Crowle and also, Gran and Granfer Julian - Ellen and Richard Julian, who owned the house.

My granfer worked on the 'Mica Drags' at the Bodelva Clay Works right up until he retired. This is the clay works on which 'The Eden Project' is now built. Just think how amazed Granfer Julian would be if he knew that the hut where he ate his pasty is under the place now known the world over.

Some days, I would walk with gran to Bodelva and take dinner down to granfer. This would often be mashed potato, bacon and fried egg in an enamel dish which gran would cover with a tea towel. We would go down the lane opposite the Chapel, through Hennals clay works and down through Restineas Farm. Granfer had a crib hut where he could sit down and have his dinner - it was quite cosy. I think there must have been a stove to boil a kettle of water for a cup of tea.

My dad worked seven days a week for his father at Carwollen Farm, Carclaze. He was always up early in the morning and did not get home again until late in the evening. He had to be at work very early as he delivered milk from the farm to Treverbyn Road and Slades Road.

Sometimes, I was able to go with him. I enjoyed this, as I met up with all the customers and was able to stay with my other grandparents, Gran and Grandad Crowle. I do not think my dad earned very much money. Both my dad and Granfer Julian cycled to work each day. Up in the village, granfer had six fields, a cow house and a barn. The six fields were rented from Mr Rundle of Tregrehan. Granfer kept three or four cows and also, had a horse and cart. It was mum's job to get up early in the morning and walk up to the fields to hand milk the cows and this was again repeated in the evening. In the morning the milk was strained into a bucket and put into bottles and sealed with cardboard tops before being delivered around the village. I went with mum most days - winter and summer! I loved sitting on a stool in the corner of the cow shed. It was so warm and cosy with the heat from the cows; so quiet and peaceful even though it was a bit smelly! Poor mum did all the hard work involved in the milking. The fields were up a lane by the side of the telephone box in the village. Mum would bring the rest of the milk back home and some would be put in a churn and collected by lorry to be taken to Lostwithiel milk factory. Gran would put the rest into an enamel pan which was put on the top of the stove to be scalded to make cream. From the cream, she would make butter which was patted into all kinds of fancy shapes. Some of the cream and butter was sold to people in the village.

At the back of the house was a field with several out-houses and a barn. Pigs were kept in one of the houses and there was always chickens running around; with the addition of turkeys at Christmas. It was gran or mum's job to kill the chicken which we ate as roasts or in pies. We always had fresh eggs.

Arthur Trevains, who lived up the hill near us, would come down and kill a pig for granfer. I did not ever see one being killed, but shall never forget the poor pig squealing, although I did enjoy all the things that gran cooked from the pig. There would be roast pork, bacon, which would have been salted in a keive (barrel), hogs pudding, tripe, brawn and pig leg pie to name but a few things! All the fat was cut up and melted down in the oven, then used for cooking.

Mum helped gran with the washing, housework and cooking. The bread was all homemade. The flour was bought in 56lb bags but didn't last very long. I remember a coal range being removed and a Rayburn installed in its place in the back kitchen. We did have electric lighting but no refrigerator, washing machine or vacuum cleaner. Neither did we have fitted carpets - only rugs and linoleum. There was carpet on the stairs held in place by brass rods. These had to be cleaned and polished regularly with 'brasso' polish.

Of course, there was no television, but we did have a good radio which granfer and dad enjoyed listening to. At the front of the house, granfer grew all kinds of vegetables. I liked to help him in the garden with my special little Cornish shovel. I wish I knew what happened to it - thrown out I expect!

All our groceries were delivered by John Penhall of Tregrehan. He would come and take the order one week and then it would be delivered the following week. Algey Jones delivered the bread from Carns Bakery; the butcher came from Kittows. Charlie Welsh delivered coal from Clemows and Mr Rowse came from Holmbush with cases of drapery that contained lace, elastic, tape, aprons and all kinds of towels. He also sold needles and cotton for sewing. Another tradesman that came was Mr Glasson with the 'Kleen-ez-y'. He brought with him all kinds of brushes and polishes.

When the evacuees came down from London, Mum went with Mrs Luke of Knightor Manor into St Austell Station to fetch the children and bring them back to the village where they were allocated different homes. We had a girl called Jean Smeeton, who I think came from Tottenham. She was a year older than me and I thought it was lovely having company. Thinking back, it must have been awful for Jean and her family to be split up.

A school was set up in the village hall for all the evacuees. The story goes that because Jean was allowed to go there, I made quite a scene and wanted to go with her. I remember going for a while. Jean must have been five years old and I about four. I have never forgotten that one of the teachers shut me in the toilet and I could not get out! At that time, I must have done something bad, but I haven't a clue what it was!

Unfortunately, when Jean went back home, we lost touch with her. I think mum did hear from her when she was in her teens and we did have a photograph from her. Gran had a lot more people staying, who came from London. They would stay, perhaps, one or two weeks and I can remember some sleeping in the front room and all the rooms upstairs would be taken up! Even the bathroom had a bed put up which I would share with Jean. We must have been much squashed up, although everyone seemed happy, together. I expect they were probably glad to have got away from all the bombing that was taking place in London!

In the 1940s, whether it was because of the war, we knew everyone in the village and it was so friendly. There was always someone popping in for a cup of tea and one of gran's yeast buns or a piece of pasty. Because everything was rationed, coupons were issued. If anyone was desperate for any particular thing, there was always someone who would help. Things were swapped around like food, clothes and toys. Mum was able to get extra coupons for shoes for me, because I had big feet!!

After the village hall school closed, I went to Carclaze Infants School which was then situated in the Sunday school. We had to walk from Trethurgy, although, sometimes, I rode on the back of my mum's bike. Then, one day, we were moved down to the proper Infants School. All the children had to help move the tables and chairs down the lane to the school. There were three classes. The teachers were Mrs Pascoe, who was the headmistress, and Miss Armstrong - I do not recall who the third teacher was! When I was in the infants, I always took a packed lunch to school and, during the morning break, had a bottle of milk. When seven years old, I went to Carclaze Junior School, which was next to the Infants. Mr Williams was the head teacher of the four classes. The classes were known as standards 1, 2, 3 and 4. At dinner time, the children who wanted to stay to eat had to walk to a Nissan hut in Robartes Place, which was the canteen. It was also used by children from Mount Charles School. We would walk to school and back every day regardless of the weather. Then, at eleven, I went to West Hill Secondary School for Girls, which I really liked. I was able to catch a school bus to get there each day.

In December 1945, my brother, Richard, was born in the 'Agatha Nursing Home' which was in a large house near Poltair School. When I got a bit older, mum would allow me to take Richard out for walks, which was a good excuse to meet up with friends. When I was twelve, Richard and I both became ill with scarlet fever. I remember, even now, the symptoms of a sore throat and feeling very hot. We had to be isolated from everyone in our bedroom and only mum could look after us. Granfer gave us a gramophone to play to keep us amused; as well as many books and comics to look at. When we were free of the infection and able to move out, all the books and papers had to be burnt and the room was sealed up and fumigated. It was not a good time for the family. Mum said that when she went anywhere, people would cross the road to avoid becoming infectious.

Our family life was mainly centred on the Methodist chapel. On Sundays, I always had to wear my very best clothes. I wasn't allowed to play around and had to be well behaved. I used to go to Sunday school in the morning and then back again for a service in the afternoon and evening. Very often, the preacher would be invited back to our house for tea. Although it might have seemed boring to have to go chapel every Sunday, at least all the boys and girls were allowed out. After chapel, a crowd of us would meet up and usually go up to the moors and Carn Grey Rock. The girls and boys of the village would often meet up with the girls and boys from Penwithick. There would be special services for Good Friday with high tea being provided. Afterwards, the children entertained everyone with a concert of Easter songs and recitations. I liked singing but I hated recitations!

After this, the next big event was the Chapel Anniversary, when the children sang in the afternoon. There was then another service in the evening when the adults sang. The following Thursday was Feast Day which everyone looked forward too! In the afternoon, there would be sports and games for the children. In the Sunday school yard, there was various sweet and fruit stalls and a brass band playing. Sometime during the afternoon, the children and their parents lined up behind the band and a person carrying the banner. We then marched up Knightor Lane to Knightor Manor, where we met Mr and Mrs. Luke and were given ice cream, which we all thought was marvellous. The last few times we had a Feast Day, we didn't have a brass band to lead us – instead, we had a loud speaker van driven by Mr French. The first thing we had at Knightor was a saffron bun and lemonade. People would come from neighbouring villages to Feast Day, making it a day to remember. We also went to other villages when it was their Feast Day.

In October, we celebrated Harvest Festival. The chapel was beautifully decorated with flowers the day before, in readiness for the special services on the Sunday. On the Sunday afternoon, all the gifts of fruit and vegetables would be brought by the children and placed on tables in the front of the chapel. There would be special services in both the afternoon and evening. On the following Tuesday, there would be a further afternoon service and tea afterwards. After tea, everyone helped to take all the gifts from the chapel into the Sunday school to be auctioned off. Mr Wilfred Keam from the village was usually the auctioneer. There would be a lot of banter with people trying to outbid each other. Bunches of grapes were very popular and seem to make the most money. My uncle, Sheldon Kingdon, would have people in fits of laughter. An example of this was when someone thought they had bought an item and Uncle Sheldon said: *"... and a tanner!"* [6d, or 2½p in decimal currency]. This would make the bidding go up and up, but it was all good hearted fun. There was always a bag or basket of apples which was put back for the children to buy at 1d each. We thought this was lovely!

At the village hall, there were various activities going on. In the war years, there was always a Christmas Party arranged for the children of the village which everyone enjoyed. I think there must have been a lot of goodies to eat, but I only remember a very large and beautifully decorated Christmas cake. This was given to us by a Mr Molyneux, who was either a director or manager of Hennals Clay Works. Anyway, the cake was gorgeous! Mrs Hicks, who lived at the top of the hill, organised games for us - it was really a happy time! Also, there were dances held in the hall quite regularly! People would come from miles around to enjoy the dancing, where there was always a live band with 'The Riviera Band' seeming to be the most popular. Bill Jane was on the piano, Ernie Jewell played the accordion and Donald Grose was on the drums. The dances would be ball-room and old-time dancing with the hall being packed with people. My mum and dad, also Mr and Mrs Hicks, would organise the drinks and refreshments. Of course, there was no licensed bar - only tea, coffee and squash! Mr and Mrs Hicks' daughter, Valerie, and I were allowed to go to the dance and join in.

When the dances became less popular, a new billiard table was installed for the men of the village. Dad enjoyed playing billiards and also, they played table tennis. I went up to the hall quite often with dad and liked to watch all that went on. The trouble was the size of the billiard table - it was so large that it spoilt any dancing. It seemed never the same again.

When I was around eight years old, granfer and gran bought me a piano. I started having lessons with Mrs Sweet from Carclaze. I had a lesson each week for one hour at her house. My mum made me practice the piano and was quite strict with me, for which I am now glad because I have had hours of enjoyment from doing so. After a while, I was able to play hymns for the Sunday school in the vestry. I played a harmonium organ which had two pedals – oh, how my legs ached! At around thirteen, I started having lessons on the chapel organ. Mrs Sweet used to come to Trethurgy on the school bus to give me lessons and then, afterwards, she would walk the two miles home. I really enjoyed playing the organ for the different services.

In 1951, Gran and Grandad Crowle retired from Carwollen Farm in Carclaze and went to live at Scredda. We then left Bay View and went to live on the farm. I cried, because I wanted to stay with gran and granfer, but I also hated moving. I still attended the chapel on Sundays and continued to play the organ until it closed.

An interview with Mrs Jean Niles by W B Shipley

Trethurgy and the surrounding area lie over the Ruby Wheal iron lode, which stretches roughly from Crinnis to Withiel. The lady to whom I am about to refer, had the misfortune to live in a property that was sited directly over an old mine working. This story was told during an interview I had with Mrs Jean Niles and her son, Philip, on 2nd February 2011.

Jean and her husband Bill, together with their young sons, Philip and Gary, lived in a semi-detached cottage at Innis Moor, Penwithick. The other half of the cottage was occupied by Mrs Wherry and Mrs Cooper, who were the mother and grandmother of Mrs Niles.

During the winter of 1963, Jean Niles and her son, Philip, were sitting in their kitchen watching an episode of the Fugitive on TV. Bill Niles was away from home that evening, as he was on night shift as a lorry driver, Gary was sleeping upstairs. Both Philip and his mother describe hearing a rustling noise rather like a very heavy shower of hailstones followed by a rumble and a loud bump. Thinking that Gary had fallen out of bed, Jean opened the door to the passage which led to the stairs to check up on him, only to discover that the passage floor had disappeared. She found herself staring into a very large cavity which extended across the width of the passage and undermined the wall of the lounge opposite. Jean had difficulty in believing what she saw! It was in fact a jumbled heap of the lounge furniture which had partly descended into a pit. Once she had recovered from the initial shock, Jean's only concern was to get the two boys and herself away from the danger.

Realising that the way upstairs was impossible, she took herself and Philip outside and went next door to her mother's home, whose immediate reaction was to tell her daughter she had been dreaming. A brief conference took place and it was decided that Jean and Philip would go to the nearest neighbour for help. Fortunately, he was there and after acquiring a ladder, he accompanied the now homeless pair back to the subsiding house. This man was a Mr Johns, more commonly known as 'Butch' Johns. He placed the ladder on the outside wall just below Gary's bedroom window and after tapping on the glass to wake the boy, managed to wrap him in a blanket and bring him safely down.

The nearest phone was about a quarter of a mile away, so 'Butch' went off to telephone the police and the English China Clay company who employed Bill Niles. When the police arrived, they were adamant that no one should remain in either of the two cottages. Therefore, the whole family moved in with Mr Johns and his wife for a few days, until they were re-housed. The following day, the fire service arrived and saved the contents of the two cottages, with exception of the furniture in the collapsed lounge that included a three-piece suite, a radiogram and a large cupboard full of bed linen. The kitchen floor had also subsided during that night, magnifying the danger that Philip and his mother had been in during the previous evening. Jean recalls that had her husband been at home rather than working that night, the family would have been in the lounge with possibly dire consequences.

At the time of this frightening occurrence, Jean was five months pregnant with her daughter, Karen, and luckily, neither of them suffered any ill effects. The loss of their home and substantial amount of their belongings was judged to be an 'Act of God' and therefore, no compensation was forthcoming, though it must be added that the properties were rented and their landlord - English Clays Lovering & Pochin, quickly re-housed them at Kerrow Moor, about two miles away.

This incident was widely reported, both in the local newspapers and also, on the television programme 'Spotlight'. No official reason was ever given for the subsidence. However, local discussion came up with a reasonable solution that, sometime previously, men working at a nearby clay pit had suddenly been inundated with a torrent of water and debris which gushed from the side of the pit. It was concluded that the working at the pit had released water from an old mine tunnel which ran under or close to the cottage and that, this sudden lessening of pressure, had caused the ground to subside. This, of course, is only surmise, but it sounds a very reasonable proposition. The end of the story is that the cottage was finally destroyed by being blown up with dynamite and the rubble was then shovelled down into the cavity.

Memories of Jackie Trudgeon

We moved to Carn Grey in 1966/67 and looked, not to St Austell, but to Trethurgy, for our social life. There were lots of children around for us to play with and our playground became the fields and clay area, from Carn Grey to Trethurgy.

The chapel played a significant part in our lives, back then, in the late sixties and early seventies. We attended Sunday school with our neighbours, Mary and Stephen Mitchell, as did most of the children in the village, so it was a chance to meet up with friends. Mr and Mrs Body would read a Bible story and then, we would have to answer questions in our exercise books. When I was deemed old enough, I would read the small children their story, in a room off the main hall. They would then draw a picture. Every year, we would be given a book which reflected how many times we had attended. I remember being pleased when I received the 'History of Kings and Queens' one year.

Being part of the Sunday school meant that come anniversaries or feast days, you were expected to perform a recitation or song in the chapel. I can see myself practicing and practicing and worrying in case I forgot my lines, but it was always alright on the day. Once, friends and I were allowed to play our recorders.

Feast Days were always something to look forward too. We all enjoyed the teas, with the tables being laid out in rows and piled with jam and cream splits. The cups, saucers and plates, as were set out on such occasions, would proudly proclaim that we were part of Trethurgy chapel.

I further remember a fete when we were bowling for a pig, but not being really sure if that was the prize! I also loved the 'beetle drives' that were held in the evenings and recall them as being packed and full of laughter.

As children, we were allowed quite a lot of freedom and roamed all over. We would walk to the post office with our pennies to buy lollipops and also, spent many hours in the quarry. My brother would fish there; whilst, every year, I would collect frog spawn for the school nature table. The empty quarry buildings were where we imagined other worlds, or tested ourselves, seeing how far we could climb or jump. I was particularly proud of being able to climb the face of the quarry in front of the rock. In 1971, we were very excited, when they filmed an episode of 'Dr Who' in the clay pit behind the farm where we lived.

The carnival was revived and the younger children all got the chance of becoming the queen or an attendant and riding around the village in an open backed van. Dancing the flora dance was a good way to end the day.

On this occasion, the feast queen was Rachel Seward and her attendants seated around her are: Kenwyn Trenberth, Matthew Luke, Donna Thom, Joanna Mugford, Beth Condon and the Grimshaw sisters.

As a student at Penrice School, we were taken to the 'round' settlement. It was the first time I had seen a 'dig' and afterwards, went to visit it several times on my own.

In 1973, my youngest brother, Jonathon, was christened in the chapel during a Sunday service. I also remember the old lady who lived in the caravan, as mum often stopped the car to chat to her or drop something off.

Living next to a clay pit, one got used to the house shaking whenever they 'blasted'. When I was seven, I came home from school with a clay pot which I was so proud of and put it on the mantlepiece. About five minutes later, the siren went off, the house shook as they blasted and my lovely pot lay in pieces on the floor!

My memories by Marjorie Hambly (nee Keam)

I have great memories of growing up in Trethurgy. We made our own entertainment and felt safe wherever we went. I remember we used to make camps on the moors and had all sorts of adventures. One of my strongest memories was climbing up the sand burrows and sliding down on pieces of cardboard! Another favourite was watching for the delivery from John Williams of waste sawdust and off-cut pieces of wood to the top quarry. With wheelbarrows at the ready, we went to rummage through the sawdust and bring home the wood for our fires.

We lived in 'Belle Vue', which was then the office of Selleck Nicholls on the ground floor and the home of Miss Katy Nicholls, who lived in the flat above. When the building was converted into flats in the late 1930s, the people who lived in the top flat were Wilfred Keam, May Keam (nee Gregory), Marjorie Keam and Kathryn Keam. In the bottom flat lived Jack and Winnie Chapman and their son, Brian. Nearby, at 'Rock Cottage' lived Howard and Margaret Darlington with their children, Sandra and Kay. Prior to that Gran Gregory, Bill Gregory and Rodney Gregory were the occupants.

My friend Sylvia and I had a great adventure one Sunday after chapel. Still wearing our best clothes, we decided to go for a walk. We ended up by going to the bottom quarry and, on climbing half way down, walked around the edge of the quarry. We thought it was great fun; but my mother saw us while looking out of the front room window at home and we were in big trouble - "Very dangerous and very stupid!" were her very words!

During the early forties, we had two evacuee boys - John and Frankie Reed from the London area living with us in Belle Vue. They were very intrigued by the country life and its customs. Each year, on the Monday after Chapel Harvest Festival, the fruit and produce were auctioned for the chapel funds. I remember Frankie's bid for everything was a 'tanner' (six-pence, in those days). Another time, mother took us to visit an old lady who lived in a cottage in the village for tea. Their remarks were "ain't it quaint and old fashion!" Great memories, those childhood days!

My early memories by Dennis Ronaldson

Trethurgy is a small village situated on the road mid-way between St Austell and Luxulyan. The village, at that time, comprised of a number of cottages and smallholdings. There was also a Methodist chapel, Sunday school and the Institute. About half a mile away was 'Knightor Manor' occupied by Hayden Luke. This was a large house with an extensive lawn that Mr Luke used to throw open on the village Feast days. The local children loved playing on the lawn and each was rewarded with a large saffron bun which was greatly enjoyed.

I was born in June 1936 at 'Box Cottage'. The cottage was situated up a lane in the centre of the village. It was a 'two up and down' with an outside lean-to. This was our wash-house and inside was a 'copper' - a large container for heating water with a fireplace underneath. This was lit for doing the wash and also, provided hot water for our bath nights. We would use a tin bath in front of the kitchen fire. The kitchen dining room was lit by a paraffin oil lamp which had a glass globe on top. All other lighting was by candles or, if in the outhouse, by a paraffin lantern. I remember that the child with the smallest hands had to clean the inside of the globe using paper. Our cooking and heating was provided by a stove which could be used as both an open fire and oven. We mostly used wood for the fire which we would collect locally. I remember that we used 'Zebo' - a black block which had to be wetted and brushed onto the stove - to make it shine.

At the time I was born, there were two other children - Lewis, who was born in 1931 and Betty, the following year. We had an outside toilet that my father had constructed and a large barrel was used to collect all the rain water from the guttering. Water was very important to us, as our only other supply came from behind Mildred Wellington's shop in the centre of the village. This water source was known as the 'shute' which was basically a pipe coming out of a cliff face. The water would be carried in buckets, sometimes for half a mile or so. It was then placed in chlome pitchers to keep it cool and fresh for drinking purposes.

Life was very hard for my father, George, and my mother, Winnie. Father was working down in the tin mines at Pool near Redruth during the war years and only came home at the weekends. I remember that because he was working in arsenic water in the mine and used to get numerous boils on his legs. One of my chores, at that time, was to hold a heated bottle on the boils to extract the core of the boil.

My dad's friend and workmate was Bill Hicks, who lived at Carn Grey. Bill was the union rep and used to call for the union dues. My mother had been forewoman at a dressmaking factory in Newquay before her marriage and one of the most overworked items in our house was a 'Singer' treadle sewing machine. She used to make most of our clothes, like our suits and dresses, right down to our school caps. She would work well into the night to complete some garments for us.

My brother, Preston, was born in 1939 and my sister, Sylvia, arrived in 1942. Looking back, I will never know how seven of us managed to live in a two-bedroomed house with no electricity, no gas or water and no mains sewerage. My father used to grow many vegetables in our large garden and had a constant supply of rabbit - I don't ever remember us going without food. I was well versed in catching rabbits and, as we always had a dog, ferrets and nets, I soon found that this could be quite profitable. I set wire traps and checked them very early in the mornings before school. I remember taking them to Northcotts Butchers in St Austell and receiving a shilling a pound for them - "Whoopee, I was rich!"

The chapel and Sunday school were very active during these years. My mother insisted that we attended Sunday school on Sunday mornings, then again at two-o-clock and finally, the evening service. After each service, we had to change from our best suits into our casual clothes to ensure that we looked smart and tidy for chapel. I remember that the chapel organ was operated by forced air which was controlled by a handle at the side of the organ and hidden by a curtain. As the air pressure increased, a small weight would lift up allowing the person pumping to judge when an adequate air pressure was achieved. This was operated by Geoffrey Liddicoat with the help of my brother, Lewis. At times, they would not concentrate and the organ would slow down causing frantic looks from the organist. I can recall various concerts being held in the Sunday school by performers from the villages around the area. I remember having to learn various recitations to recite at anniversaries, harvest festivals and other occasions. I remember, one time during the war, I was told to go to the chapel and tell Winnie Chapman to go home right away, as a telegram had arrived for her. If my memory serves me right, it was notifying her that her husband, Jack, who was in the Navy, was missing. Apparently his boat had been sunk. Sad, sad days! I can recall, seeing the flashes of bombs dropping on Plymouth early on in the war. We had to strictly adhere to the blackout laws, with blankets being placed inside of the windows to ensure that no light could be seen from the outside. In this way, the Germans could not identify where they were. This was a time of ration books and severe shortages of foodstuffs. Our grocer, John Penhall from Tregrehan, used to call twice a week. I recall my mother making out two shopping lists – one which she needed and one that she could afford. Mr Penhall would then deliver the goods in his Austin van - one of the very few vehicles seen in the village at that time - on his next visit. I often walked to Tregrehan to collect some item that she was short of. We got our milk from Sheldon Kingdon who had a farm in the village. He used to travel around on a pony and trap with the milk churns on the back fitted with taps. His wife was Ernestine and he had two daughters and a son, Geoffrey. Shirley was his eldest daughter and she would be heard many a late night herding the cows home for milking, as she drove them through the village.

My first school was set up at the Institute when I was five years old. This was only a temporary arrangement and when it closed down sometime afterwards, I was transferred to Carclaze School. The headmaster was Mr Williams and the headteacher, Mrs Armstrong. This entailed a two mile walk along Carn Grey in all winds and weathers and I recall being blown off my feet on many occasions. I also remember being banned from the dancing classes due to the fact that my hob nail boots were the only footwear capable of standing up to those journeys. I have thus dreaded dancing all my life! I remained at Carclaze until I was eleven years old and was then transferred to West Hill Primary School in St Austell. This meant a three and a half mile walk each way. The infants at Trethurgy were provided with a taxi for school at the end of the war and we were very envious when it sailed past us each day. My brother, Lewis, and sister, Betty, went to Tregrehan School at that time. At school, I excelled at science and metalwork and very little else!!! After a life time in engineering, I think the seeds were sown during this period.

Looking back, I think we were very poor in financial terms; but very rich in experiences that left me with a strong sense of survival. I also think we had the best playground in the world; with two quarries, many pools, acres of moorland and numerous friends who were in much the same situation as me. To name a few: Michael Bennett, Barrie Shipley, Fernley Baker, Tommy Crocker, Norman Crocker, Henry and Maurice Sloggett, Leslie Rowse and Bill Trevains. Many youthful hours were spent in the quarries, playing on rafts which we had made from any pieces of wood that we could find. There was an aggregate crusher situated near the top quarry. This was a huge structure and we would spend many hours climbing to the top and seeing a wonderful view of the village and surrounding areas; right down to the coast at Fowey. I used to think that this place was the top of the world and cannot ever recall being bored. The crusher was removed, I think, to provide steel for the war effort, as were many railings in the area. I remember the American soldiers being in the area and based in the bottom quarry. They used to ride around the village on horseback and bicycles.

My early memories by Alec Hambly

On August 24th 1937, I was born at Carne Cross, Starrick Moor, which lies between Trethurgy and Luxulyan. I had relatives at Chytan Farm in Trethurgy - my Aunt Gert and Uncle Silvanus Ford and their daughter, Marion. Uncle Charles Hambly also lived there and worked on the farm.

On the way to Garker was a small holding called *'Ikes'* although I never knew the reason why! My mother's sister and her husband lived there, with their four children.

My schooling started at the institute. I was taken there by my cousin Marion and later, was joined by my cousin, Terry Higgins, from 'Ikes'. The institute ceased to function as a school in May 1944 and we were sent to Carclaze junior school to which we had to walk.

At that time, feast days were celebrated in Trethurgy on Thursdays and we were given the afternoon off. At 2-o-clock, we would be taken by the Bugle bus to Carluddon; from there, we walked across the moors passing Penhedra and Alseveor farms on the way. We ran down the bumpy lane to Trethurgy and joined up with the others at the Sunday school. We then marched to Knightor Manor and returned to the Sunday school for tea and sports in the field opposite. There was also a Sunday school Christmas party which we enjoyed. It was provided by the Lantern China Clay works at Hennals. The owners, Mr Morley and Mr Molyneaux, whom I remember as being a very tall gentleman, each attended every other Christmas.

We enjoyed the freedom to play on the moors and our adventure playground was the top quarry. Once in a while, when the bottom quarry was drained, we could walk in to explore and look at the old machinery. No health and safety rules in those days!

Appendix A - *Past local newspaper reports*

October 1795

CORNWALL.

TO be LEASED for 99 years, if three persons to be nam d by the purchaser shall so long live, All that MESSUAGE and TENEMENT, called The GULLIES, situate in Trethurgey, in the parish of St. Austell, in the said county, and now in the occupation of —— Williams, widow, and Robert Keam ; consisting of a dwelling house, barn, and stable, and upwards of four acres and half of good land.

For which purpose a Survey will be held at the house of John Robins, innkeeper, in St. Blazey, on Monday the 23d day of November next, by three o'clock in the afternoon.

For a view of the premises apply to the occupiers ; and for further particulars to Mr. Hearle, attorney at law, in St. Columb, in the said county.

N. B. If the premises are not leased, a Survey will then be held for Letting them at an yearly rent.

Dated October 28, 1795.   530

June 1857

BOND'S TENEMENT.

Situate at Trethurgy, in the Parish of St. Austell, in the County of Cornwall, consisting of a substantial Dwelling-house, Barn, Mowhay, and about 7 Acres (statute Measure) of Arable, Meadow, and Pasture Land, now in the occupation of Mr. Thomas Reed, as Tenant thereof, from year to year.

Lot 7.—The Fee Simple and Inheritance of and in all that newly-erected COTTAGE, situate at Trethurgy aforesaid, now in the occupation of Mr. William Borlase, as Tenant thereof, from year to year, at the yearly rent of £3 10s.

Lot 8.—The Fee-simple and Inheritance of and in all that COTTAGE, situate at Trethurgy aforesaid, now in the occupation of Mr. John Stephens as Tenant thereof, from year to year, at the yearly rent of £2 10s.

The above Estates will be found desirable Investments : Lower Menedue is a good Grazing Farm, distant about 3½ miles from St. Blazey, 6 miles from Bodmin, 5 miles from St. Austell, and within half a mile of a Station on the Treffry Railway to Par, which affords great facilities for obtaining Manures, and transmitting Agricultural Produce ; Bond's Tenement is 2½ miles from St. Austell, and the like distance from St. Blazey, and is well adapted for a Currier, as it lies contiguous to several large Iron Mines and Clay Works. The Cottages offer inducements to parties having small sums at command.

For viewing the several Lots, apply to the respective Tenants ; and for any further information to Mr. WALTER HICKS, St. Austell - Mr. R. W. CHILDS, Solicitor, 25, Coleman-street, London ; or to

Messrs. COODE, SONS and SHILSON, Solicitors, St. Austell, Cornwall.

Dated St. Austell, 26th May, 1857.

February 1877

ST. AUSTELL.

BURGLARY AT TRETHURGY.— Recently about 12 o'clock at night a smash was heard at the window of a small shop, kept by a poor widow. On coming down stairs to see what was the matter, it was found that the window had been broken in and a quantity of goods taken from inside. It is generally considered that an attempt was made to get at the till, but this not being accessible the goods were taken instead of cash. The poor woman screamed for help, but there was none at hand, and the burglar or burglars got safe off. There are several roughs about this neighbourhood, who may be found out with dogs and guns at night time, and the police should keep a sharp eye upon them.

February 1883

THE fortnightly meeting of the Board of Guardians was held on Friday. Sir C. B. Graves-Sawle, Bart., in the chair. The medical officer, Dr. Mason, reported that two deaths had occurred at Trethurgy from diphtheria. Proper precautions had been taken to prevent the spreading of the disease. The Chairman reported that he had visited the Mount Charles and Charlestown water works, with the other members of the committee and that they discovered that the joints of the conducting pipe were very badly made and that the reservoir was leaking. They recommended that the joints of the pipe should be recemented, and that a gutter drain be placed around the reservoir. The Board instructed the surveyor, Mr. Samble, to proceed with the work at once.

January 1891

FATAL ICE ACCIDENT NEAR ST. AUSTELL.—An inquest was held on Friday, by Mr. E. G. Hamley, county coroner, into the death of William Frederick Hore Payne, who was drowned whilst skating at Trethurgy on Wednesday. The verdict was "Death from accidental drowning."

PETTY SESSIONS.—These sessions were held on Tuesday, before Mr. R. G. Lakes (chairman), Mr. T. Hext, and Mr. A. Coode. Laura Rowett summoned Wm. H. Solomon for assaulting her at Mevagissey, and was fined 5s. and costs. W. L. Hawke was summoned for allowing two donkeys to stray on the highway at Polgooth, and was fined 1s. and costs. Richard Grose, of Roche, was fined 1s. and costs for allowing his waggon to be used without having his name on it. Wm. Pearce was fined 2s. 6d. and costs for riding on his waggon at Charlestown without having reins. Henry Crowle was fined 10s. and costs for being an improper distance from his waggon at Trenague, in St. Stephens. John L. Williams, of Nansladron, St. Ewe, was fined 2s. 6d. and costs for leaving his waggon on the highway at Nansladron. S. M. Stephens, W. H. Davey, both of Tregony, W. H. Trudgeon, of St. Stephens, James Floyd, of Trethurgy, St. Austell, were each fined 10s. and costs, and Wm. Clemo, of St. Austell, £1 1s. and costs, for being drunk and disorderly. R. Clemes, W. Penhale, W. Grigg, and W. Goodge were summoned for allowing their cattle to stray, and were fined 1s. and costs. John Richards (a boy) was fined 5s. and costs, or seven days' imprisonment, for assaulting Wm. Dennis Jenkin at the Wesleyan Chapel-yard, St. Austell. William Hares, of St. Stephens, was summoned for damaging the grass in a field occupied by J. Martin; fined 2s. 6d. and costs with 1s. for damage, or seven days' imprisonment.

ST. AUSTELL.

FATAL ACCIDENT.—An inquest was held on Thursday at Trethurgy, St. Austell, by Mr. Preston J. Wallis, deputy-coroner, with reference to the death of Richard Luke, a clay labourer, at the Goonamarth Clay Works, on the previous day. From the evidence given it appears that the deceased was engaged with others in removing burden. Two men were above and Luke below, and the ground being of a sandy or loose character, a quantity fell and completely covered him. He got his head free, but received severe internal injuries from which he died. The jury returned a verdict of "Accidental death."

February 1883

all of Probus, for being drunk and disorderly at Grampound, were fined 10s. each and costs.—John Kingdon, of Tretburgy, was fined 2s. 6d. and costs for overloading with china-clay, a one-horse cart having over 30cwt.—Samuel Hawke, of West Hill,

February 1892

each respectively.—Mrs. Mary Sandercombe charged Mrs. Sarah Luke, of Tretburgy, with setting fire to a furze fence on February 28th. Mr. W. J. Graham appeared for the complainant, and Mr. J. E. G. Sandford for defendant. The evidence (as narrated by a large number of witnesses on either side) proved to be a of very conflicting nature, and the case was dismissed. —Henry Beard claimed £1 18s. from Henry Skidgmore, of Treray, St. Stephens-in-Branwell, wages due to him. Skidgmore was ordered to pay the amount, with costs.—R. T. Richards, landlord of the King's Head Inn,

July 1894

KNIGHTOR AND TRENOWETH FARM, ST. AUSTELL.

TO be LET, by TENDER, from year to year (or for a term of 7 years as may be arranged), with immediate possession,

KNIGHTOR AND TRENOWETH FARM, situate near Tretburgy, about 2 miles from the market town of St. Austell, consisting of an excellent farm house, two workmen's cottages, and commodious outbuildings, and about 87 acres of good arable and pasture land, for many years in the occupation of Mr. William Nicholls.

The farm may be seen on Mondays, Wednesdays, and Saturdays, on application to Mr. F. H. NICHOLLS, at Knightor, and further particulars and conditions of letting may be obtained of

Messrs. CARLYON AND STEPHENS,
Solicitors, St. Austell,

by whom alternative Tenders (to include the tithe Rent-charges, apportioned at £9 9s. 9d. yearly), will be received until and inclusive of the 28th day of July, 1894.

The highest or any tender not necessarily accepted.

Dated St. Austell, July 12. 1894.

KNIGHTOR, ST. AUSTELL.

Unreserved Sale of Horses, Waggons, Farm Stock, Implements of Husbandry, &c.

HANCOCK and SONS have received instructions from the Trustees of the Estate of Mr. William Nicholls. to SELL by AUCTION, at KNIGHTOR, near Trethurgy, in the parish of St. Austel, on THURSDAY, the 7th day of June, 1894, the undermentioned

HORSES AND WAGGONS:—

10 strong and powerful horses for the clay carrying, 5 clay waggons, complete sets of harness for the teams of horses, waggon covers.

FARM STOCK:—

5 milch cows, 4 yearling steers, 1 yearling heifer, 1 calf, 5 heifers, 1 heifer (in calf), 4 steers, 33 ewes, 41 lambs, 27 hoggets, 3 horses.

IMPLEMENTS OF HUSBANDRY, &c.—1 spring market trap, 4 carts, harness, 1 hay turner (Michelson's), 1 Samuelson's combined reaper and mower, grass seed sower, 1 double plough, 1 single plough, winnowing machine, 1 chiseler, 1 horse hoe, 1 roller, chaff cutter, pigs' troughs, wheelbarrow, pikes, dung forks, hutches, whips, breeching, caps and posts, galvanized iron sheets, ladders, grinding stone, scythes, vice, diggers, hoes, shovels, &c., &c.

GRASS FOR HAY.—5 fields of grass for hay, about 12 acres.

Sale to commence at 12 o'clock noon prompt.

The whole of the above will be positively sold without reserve.

Dated St. Austell, May 30th, 1894.

Taken from the Cornish Guardian of 28 April 1916

TRETHURGY.

Mr. Eddie Burt has, we understand, been killed in action in France. He is the first from Trethurgy to lay down his life for King and country. Great sympathy is extended to his parents and family.

The anniversary of the Wesleyan Band of Hope was held on Good Friday. In the afternoon a children's service was given under the leadership of Miss Nicholls, the organist. Following a tea for the children a public tea was provided, supervised by Bro. R. B. Higman, Mrs. Nicholls, Mrs. T. Bassett, Mrs. Morcom, Mrs. Dewings, and Miss Nicholls. In the evening a service of song was rendered by the choir, the readings being given by Mr. Jas. Floyd. The president of the Band of Hope (Mr. T. Bassett) presided.

Mr Eddie Burt of Trethurgy who was killed in action in the 1st World War.

The medals awarded to Private Eddie Burt. On left - 1915 Star (for France); in the middle - British War Medal; and to the right - Victory Medal.

April 1955

Taken from the Cornish Guardian

Tragedy in Trethurgy

On Friday 22nd April 1955, tragedy struck the normally peaceful village. A fire completely destroyed Trethurgy Cottage in the early hours of the morning and unfortunately, resulting in the death of Mary Tregigga, who lived alone in the cottage; as did her neighbour Mrs Ronaldson who was rescued from her house.

The fire was discovered by Mr. T J Chapman on his way to work at 5.45a.m, when he glanced out of his car and noticed smoke pouring from Mrs Tregigga's cottage. On driving over, he found the house ablaze and seeing the fire was out of control he thought of the neighbour, Mrs Ronaldson. Rousing nearby neighbour, Mr Russell Golley, the two men summoned the fire brigade and then set about the task of rescuing Mrs Ronaldson.

Mr Chapman managed to get through a window and found the lady in an upstairs room. After carrying her downstairs in the smoke filled house, she was taken to her son's house to recover. The firemen arrived at the scene within thirteen minutes, but were unable to save Trethurgy Cottage. However, the adjoining cottage suffered limited damage to the roof timbers and some of the first floor.

Appendix B - Referrals to the water supply in Trethurgy

We take our supply of water for granted these days. However, looking back almost one hundred years, it is obvious that a great deal of effort was expended in getting it to us.

The information, below, was gathered from minutes of meetings of the St Austell Rural District Council and Water Committee from 1919 to 1936.

1919: 04 July

A letter was read from Mrs Nicholls, stating that the Trethurgy China Clay works had diverted a stream of water, which had been used for many years by the inhabitants of Trethurgy as a supply for domestic purposes. It was reported that Mr. H. S. Hancock, agent for Messrs. Gill and Ivimey, who own the stream of water, was taking action in this matter and it was decided to defer the subject pending this.

1922: 01 December

Your committee have authorised an extension of the water main to Carn Grey from Kelly's corner and Trethurgy at an estimated cost of £916/10/-. This scheme is being submitted as an unemployment scheme.

1925: 18 January

Recommend an extension of the one inch water main to Trethurgy at a cost of £34/18/-. The local inhabitants to do the work and the council to supply the materials.

1926: 19 March

CARN GREY TRETHURGY AND CARLUDDON WATER SUPPLY
A letter was read from a Mr. W. C. Hicks complaining of serious shortage of water in this area. The matter was referred to the St. Austell Water Committee with power to act.

1926: 16 July

The shortage of water at Carn Grey was discussed and it was agreed that the Slades water supply would be shut off from 1pm to 4pm.

Should this prove to be unsatisfactory, the committee would further consider the matter.

1930: 06 June

Mr. W. C. Hicks again drew attention to the inadequate supply of water to Carn Grey and Trethurgy. It was decided to regulate the water valves to increase the supply.

1931: 12 May

There is yet another complaint from Mr. Hicks, but this time, he only mentions the poor supply of water to Carn Grey.

1933: 15 August

In a report from St. Austell R.D.C., there were letters from P. Julyan and S Tonkin applying for the extension of supply from the mains at Trethurgy to Alseveor farm and Pentruff cottage. This was referred to the water committee.

1936: 12 May

Mr P. Julyan again asked for an extension of the water main to his premises at Alseveor. This request was refused.

[The Mr. Hicks, as mentioned above, can be seen in the photograph of the official 'opening' of the Institute.]

Appendix C - Old Maps of Trethurgy

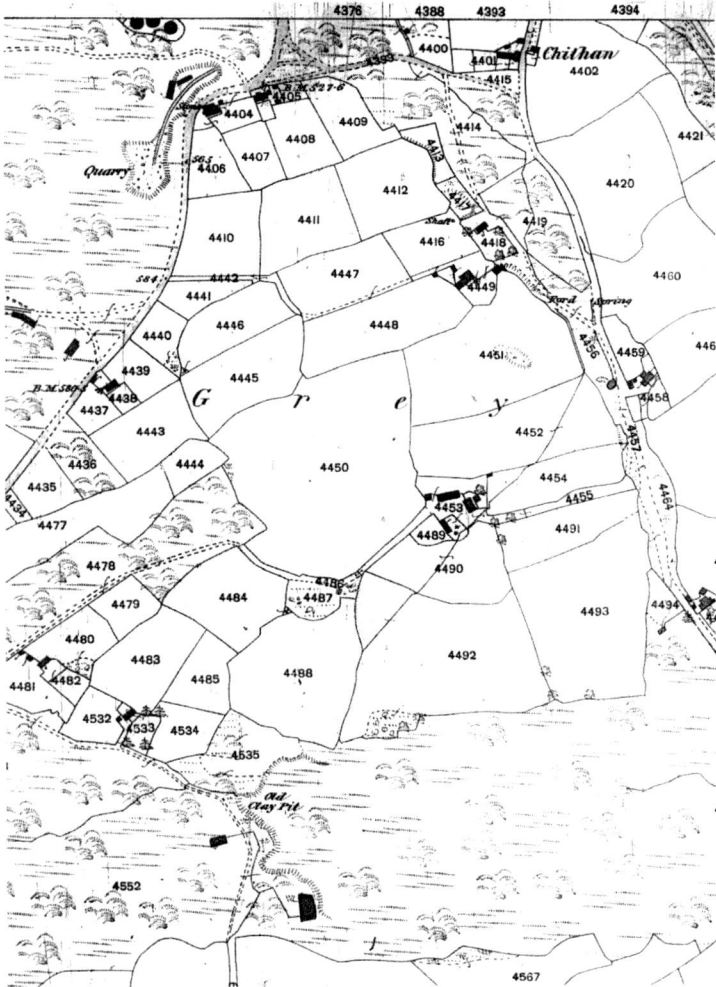

Reference: Ordnance Survey Map 1882

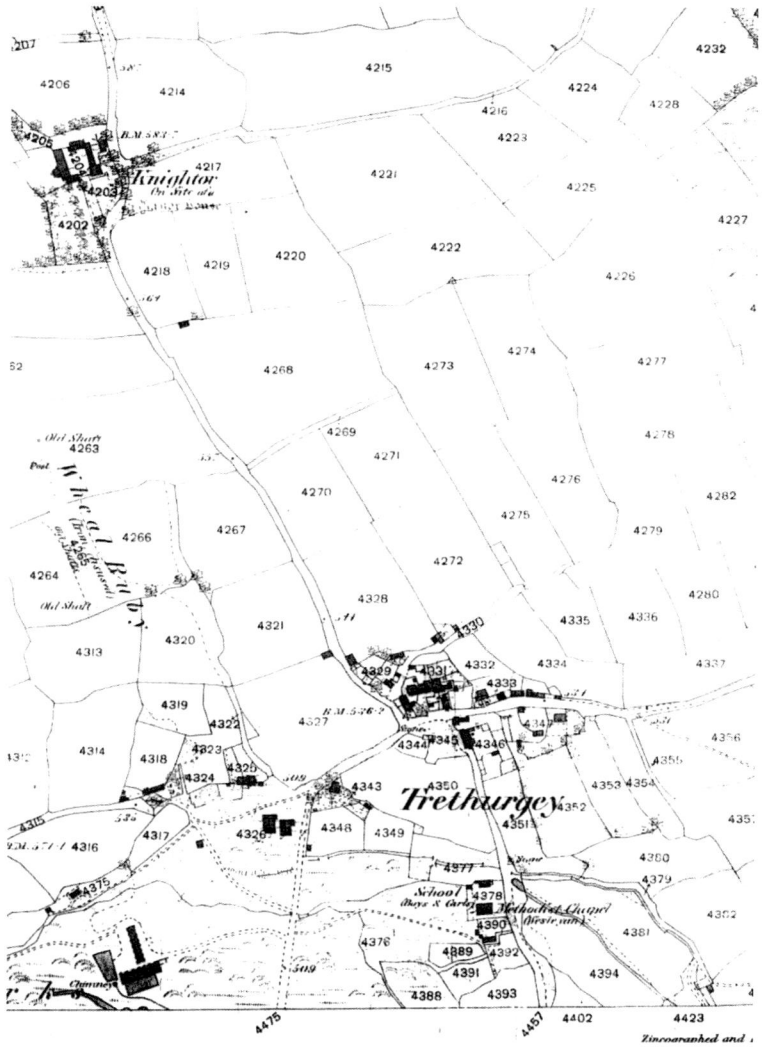

Reference: Ordnance Survey Map 1882

Part of 1842 Tithe map with details of Land ownership, tenancy and use

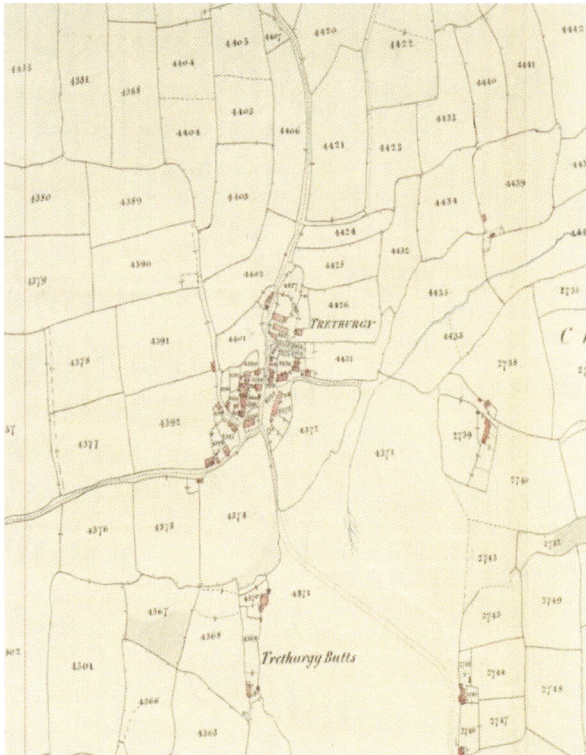

Reference: TM/8 - Courtesy of Cornwall Record Office

Trethurgy Butts

Landowner	Duke of Cornwall and John Snell (lessee)
Occupier	William Soby
Reference numbers	4368 arable field, 4369 and 4370 house and garden.

Landowner /Occupier   Duke of Cornwall and John Butterworth Trevanion
Innis Moor
4451, 4452, 4453, 4469, 4479 and 4542 - rough pasture

Landowner /Occupier   David Ezekial / Robert Stephens
The Veals
4377, 4378, 4391, 4392 - arable land
4385 / 4386   Lower and Higher Brake
4387 / 4388   Lower and upper Grandmothers Park
4389 / 4390   Outer and Inner Tinners Meadow

Landowner/Occupier	Mary Hancock 4422 Two Plots, 4428 Dwelling House 4450 Outer Field
Landowner/Occupier	Richard Julyan 4423 Crooked Meadow, 4439 Homer Close, 4441 Long Close, 4444 Hill, 4445 Hill Field, 4446 Higher Hill
Landowner/Occupier	Joseph Coombe 4396 House and garden
Landowner/Occupier	Thomas Stephens 4397 House and garden
Landowner/Occupier	Richard Luke 4308 House and garden
Landowner/Occupier	Thomas Reed 4400 House and garden
Landowner/Occupier	William Perry 4393 Trethurgy Chapel
Landowner/Occupier	Robert Stephens 4379 Great Field, 4380, 4381 acre and half, 4382 half acre, 4383 Brake, 4384 Moor, 4385 Dwelling House (Mowhay)
Landowner/ Occupier	Walter Hicks / Thomas Reed 4402 Mowhay Meadow, 4404 Orchard Meadow, 4405 Higher Barnes Close, 4406 Lenley Park, 4407 Garden
Landowner/Occupier	Richard Julyan / Nicholas Hore 4394 Dwelling House
Landowner/Occupier	John Trevanion / Charles Butterworth / Richard Julyan 4367 Butts Field, 4412 Moors, 4416 The Hill, 4418 Shutty Close, 4420 Hally Vean, 4421 Barn Town, 4424 Little Meadow, 4426 Under Town, 4434 Chetan
Field,	4436 Henowls Moor, 4437 Stitch, 4438 Rocky Close, 4440 Hay Meadow, 4442 Bush Barn, 4443
Landowner/Occupier	Thomas Snell 4429 Dwelling House, 4432 End Alls Meadow, 4433 Crooked Meadow, 4435 End Alls Moor, 4413 Moors, 4414 Clover Field, 4415 Hill Meadow, 4417 Lower Stutty Close, 4419 Stutty Close, 4425 Matthews Meadow, 4430 Town Place, 4431 Old Walls, Higher Hills, 4449 Lower Hill

Reference: TA/8 - Courtesy of Cornwall Record Office

Appendix D - 1851 census of Trethurgy residents

Location	Name	Age	Occupation
Alseveor	George Morcom	53	Farmer(12acres)
	Ann Morcom	50	
	William Morcom	25	
	Thomas Morcom	23	Tin miner
	Merria Morcom	20	Tin miner
	Mary Ann Morcom	17	
	John Morcom	15	
	Richard Morcom	13	
Butts	Robert Hore	46	Tin streamer
	Elizabeth Hore	43	
	John Hore	15	Tin mine lab
	Robert Hore	13	Tin mine lab
	Jane Hore	10	Scholar
	Joseph Hore	8	
	Merria Hore	5	
	William Hore	3	
	Philip Pascoe	50	Tin miner
	Julya Pascoe	49	
	Richard Pascoe	20	Stone lab
	Joseph Pascoe	17	Tin streamer
	Mary Pascoe	11	Scholar
	Martha Pascoe	11	Scholar
	Henry Pascoe	8	Scholar
	Grace Pascoe	6	Scholar
Trethurgy	Joseph Luke	29	Tin streamer
	Johanna Luke	30	
	Merria Luke	5	
	Willaim Luke	2	
	John Gilbard	28	
	Nicholas Hore	43	Copper miner
	Elizabeth Hore	38	
	Jacob Hore	13	Mine lab
	Nicholas Hore	11	
	John Hore	8	
	Jane Hore	6	
	Harriet Hore	4	
	Mary Hore	10 mths	

Trethurgy (cont.)	Elizabeth Coombe	56	Pauper
	John Coombe	25	Copper miner
	Walter Coombe	23	Copper miner
	Nicholas Coombe	19	Copper miner
	Richard Luke	65	Pauper
	Dorothy Luke	62	Pauper
	William Luke	27	Mine lab
	Merria Luke	25	
	Richard Luke	23	Tin miner
	Mary Luke	20	Tin mine lab
	Ann Julyan(lodger)	81	Pauper
	Thomas Reed	51	Farmer (10 acres)
	Mary Ann Reed	55	
	John Reed	33	Tin miner
	Thomas Reed	22	
	John Stephens	41	Tin miner
	Sarah Stephens	36	
	Mary Stephens	12	Scholar
	Sarah Stephens	8	Scholar
	Catherine Stephens	5	
	John Stephans	2	
	Thomas Philips	44	Miner
	Mary Philips	40	
	Mary Philips	11	Scholar
	John Philips	9	Scholar
	William Philips	7	
	Anna Philips	3	
	Lebaish Philips	9 mths	
	Daniel Brokenshire	41	Tin miner
	Eliza Brokenshire	41	
	Jane Brokenshire	17	Tin mine lab
	Ann Brokenshire	14	Tin mine lab
	Martha Brokenshire	8	
	Grace Brokenshire	5	